Art Through
Children's Literature

Art Through Children's Literature

Creative Art Lessons for Caldecott Books

Written and illustrated

by

Debi Englebaugh

Teacher Ideas Press
A Division of
Libraries Unlimited, Inc.
Englewood, Colorado
1994

To Robert, Taylor, and Morgan

TEACHER IDEAS PRESS
A Division of
Libraries Unlimited, Inc.
P.O. Box 6633
Englewood, CO 80155-6633
1-800-237-6124

Library of Congress Cataloging-in-Publication Data

Englebaugh, Debi.
    Art through children's literature : creative art lessons for
Caldecott books / Debi Englebaugh.
      xvi, 199 p. 22x28 cm.
      Includes bibliographical references.
      ISBN 1-56308-154-7
      1. Art--Study and teaching (Elementary)--United States.
2. Children's literature--Illustrations. 3. Caldecott Medal.
I. Title.
N362.E54   1994
372.5'2044--dc20   94-22232
                                     CIP

Contents

Introduction xiii

1—PENCIL 1
   Abraham Lincoln (d'Aulaire and d'Aulaire) 2
      Log Cabin 2
   Ashanti to Zulu: African Traditions (Musgrove) 3
      Contour Line Trees 3
   Baboushka and the Three Kings (Robbins) 4
      Village 4
   The Big Snow (Hader and Hader) 5
      Drawing with an Eraser 5
   Black and White (Macaulay) 6
      Subtle Changes 6
   Hey, Al (Yorinks) 7
      Bird Drawing 7
      Boxed Room 8
   Madeline's Rescue (Bemelmans) 9
      Architectural Landmarks 9
      Faces 10
   May I Bring a Friend? (de Regniers) 11
      Doorways 11
   Mei Li (Handforth) 12
      Neighborhood Map 12
   They Were Strong and Good (Lawson) 13
      Sky and Tree Drawings 13
      Sky with Value Changes 14
   Tuesday (Wiesner) 15
      Drawing Frogs 15

2—CRAYON 17
   Animals of the Bible, A Picture Book (Fish) 18
      Leaf Drawing with Contrast 18
      Leaf Rubbing 19
      Value Sky Drawing 20
   Cinderella, or the Little Glass Slipper (Perrault) 21
      Coach Design 21
   Drummer Hoff (Emberley) 22
      Kahbahbloom Drawing 22
      Uniforms with Patterns 23

2—CRAYON (continued)

Duffy and the Devil (Zemach) 24
   Witches Gathering 24
Fables (Lobel) 25
   Seashore 25
The Fool of the World and the Flying Ship (Ransome) 26
   Palace Drawing 26
Frog Went A-Courtin' (Langstaff) 27
   Wedding Guest 27
The Funny Little Woman (Mosel) 28
   Two Worlds 28
The Girl Who Loved Wild Horses (Goble) 29
   Geometric Blankets 29
   Symmetrical Sun Design 31
The Glorious Flight: Across the Channel
       with Louis Blériot ((Provensen and Provensen) . . 33
   Buildings in the City of Cambrai 33
Grandfather's Journey (Say) 34
   Portrait 34
Hey, Al (Yorinks) 35
   Paradise Drawing 35
The Little House (Burton) 36
   Landscape Drawing 36
   Little House at Night 37
   Seasons 38
Make Way for Ducklings (McCloskey) 39
   Buildings 39
   Duck Drawing 40
   Island Drawing 41
May I Bring a Friend? (de Regniers) 42
   Castle 42
Mei Li (Handforth) 43
   Dragon Hills 43
Nine Days to Christmas (Ets and Labastida) 44
   Pinata at Night 44
One Fine Day (Hogrogian) 45
   Sunset Drawing 45
Owl Moon (Yolen) 46
   Landscape Drawing 46
Ox-Cart Man (Hall) 47
   Town of Portsmouth 47
The Polar Express (Van Allsburg) 48
   North Pole at Night 48
Prayer for a Child (Field) 49
   Peaceful Drawing 49
Song of the Swallows (Politi) 50
   Spring Garden 50

3—MARKER 51

Always Room for One More (Leodhas) 52
   Figures 52
Cinderella, or the Little Glass Slipper (Perrault) 53
   Cinderella Drawing 53
   Stepsister Drawing 54
Duffy and the Devil (Zemach) 55
   Devil with a Shadow 55
Finders Keepers (Will and Nicolas) 56
   Line Drawing 56
The Fool of the World and the Flying Ship (Ransome) 57
   Decorative Column 57
Frog Went A-Courtin' (Langstaff) 58
   Bumblebee Drawing 58
   Cat Drawing 59
Owl Moon (Yolen) 60
   Owl Drawing 60
They Were Strong and Good (Lawson) 61
   Factory Drawing 61
Where the Wild Things Are (Sendak) 62
   Bedroom Forest 62
   Fantasy Animals 63

4—COLORED PENCIL 65

Abraham Lincoln (d'Aulaire and d'Aulaire) 66
   Map Design 66
   Sunset Drawing 67
Saint George and the Dragon (Hodges) 68
   Dragon Letters 68
   View from a Window 69
Song and Dance Man (Ackerman) 70
   Colored-Pencil Silhouette 70
   Everyday Object 71
   Staircase Drawing 72

5—CHALK 73

The Glorious Flight: Across the Channel
   with Louis Blériot (Provensen and Provensen) 74
   Lost in the Fog 74
Lon Po Po: A Red-Riding Hood Story from China (Young) 75
   Blended-Chalk Design 75
   Chalk Landscape Drawing 76
   Crayon-and-Chalk Shadow Drawing 77
Nine Days to Christmas (Ets and Labastida) 78
   Buildings at Night 78

5—CHALK (*continued*)

   The Polar Express (Van Allsburg) 79
      Christmas Ornament 79
      Polar Express on the Mountain 80
   Sylvester and the Magic Pebble (Steig) 81
      Sylvester in the Cool Night 81

6—STENCILS 83
   Ashanti to Zulu: African Traditions (Musgrove) 84
      Positive and Negative Map Design 84
   The Big Snow (Hader and Hader) 85
      Rainbow Around the Moon 85
      Snow-Covered Pines 86
   Black and White (Macaulay) 87
      Cows at Night 87
   Jumanji (Van Allsburg) 88
      Three-Dimensional Drawing 88
      Three-Dimensional Drawing with Details 89
      Three-Dimensional House 90
   The Rooster Crows (Petersham and Petersham) 91
      Cloud Rubbings 91
      Mountain Design 92
   Shadow (Cendrars) 93
      Smoke Design 93
   Why Mosquitoes Buzz in People's Ears (Aardema) 94
      Animals with Patterned Markings 94

7—COLLAGE 95
   Arrow to the Sun (McDermott) 96
      Geometric Collage 96
      Mosaic Collage 97
   Ashanti to Zulu: African Traditions (Musgrove) 98
      Landscape Collage 98
   Baboushka and the Three Kings (Robbins) 99
      Three Kings 99
   Black and White (Macaulay) 100
      Word Collage 100
   The Egg Tree (Milhous) 101
      Border Designs 101
      Positive and Negative Egg 102
   Fables (Lobel) 103
      Flowers 103
   The Fool of the World and the Flying Ship (Ransome) 104
      View from the Sky 104

Grandfather's Journey (Say) 105
   Desert-Rock Collage 105
   Torn-Paper Landscape 106
May I Bring a Friend? (de Regniers) 107
   Animal Shapes 107
Mei Li (Handforth) 108
   Chinese Architecture 108
Mirette on the High Wire (McCully) 109
   Shadow Collage 109
Nine Days to Christmas (Ets and Labastida) 110
   Newspaper Collage 110
Ox-Cart Man (Hall) 111
   Village Collage 111
Prayer for a Child (Field) 112
   Face Collage 112
   Name Design 113
Saint George and the Dragon (Hodges) 114
   Floral Panel 114
Shadow (Cendrars) 115
   Face-and-Flame Collage 115
   Shadow Design 116
The Snowy Day (Keats) 117
   Cotton Collage 117
   Simplified-Shape Collage 118
Tuesday (Wiesner) 119
   Flying Frogs 119
Where the Wild Things Are (Sendak) 121
   Wild Thing 121
Why Mosquitoes Buzz in People's Ears (Aardema) 122
   Animal Collage 122
   Pattern Snakes 123

8—WATERCOLOR 125

Duffy and the Devil (Zemach) 126
   Watercolor Window 126
Fables (Lobel) 127
   Candy Dream 127
The Funny Little Woman (Mosel) 128
   World of the Oni 128
The Girl Who Loved Wild Horses (Goble) 129
   Moon over the Hills 129
Many Moons (Thurber) 130
   Castle with Fireworks 130
   Moon Painting 131
Mirette on the High Wire (McCully) 132
   Illuminated Light 132
   Sky Painting 133

8—WATERCOLOR *(continued)*

Noah's Ark (Spier) 134
    Ark in the Rain 134
    Sequence of Events 135
    Sunset Painting 136
One Fine Day (Hogrogian) 137
    Landscape Painting 137
Owl Moon (Yolen) 138
    Moonlit Night Painting 138
Sylvester and the Magic Pebble (Steig) 139
    Crayon-Resist Sky 139
Time of Wonder (McCloskey) 140
    Moon After the Storm 140
    Morning Fog 141
    Watercolor Rain Painting 142

9—TEMPERA PAINT 143

Always Room for One More (Leodhas) 144
    Sponge Painting 144
    Value Painting 145
The Biggest Bear (Ward) 146
    Scratch-Art Bear 146
    Sponge Trees 147
Chanticleer and the Fox (Cooney) 148
    Leaves with Shadows 148
    Thatched Cottage 149
    White-Crayon Etching 150
Drummer Hoff (Emberley) 151
    Soldier Painting 151
Finders Keepers (Will and Nicolas) 152
    Scratch-Art Design 152
The Glorious Flight: Across the Channel
      with Louis Blériot (Provensen and Provensen) 153
    Airplane Painting 153
The Little Island (MacDonald) 154
    Stormy Sea 154
Madeline's Rescue (Bemelmans) 155
    Night Painting 155
Once a Mouse (Brown) 156
    Hiding in the Trees 156
One Fine Day (Hogrogian) 157
    Forest Painting with Sponge 157
Ox-Cart Man (Hall) 158
    Cotton-Swab Painting 158
The Rooster Crows (Petersham and Petersham) 159
    Cloud Design 159
A Tree Is Nice (Udry) 160
    Tree Painting with Warm Colors 160

White Snow, Bright Snow (Tresselt) 161
    Snowy Night 161

10—COLOR MIXING 163

Arrow to the Sun (McDermott) 164
    Monochromatic Design 164
The Biggest Bear (Ward) 165
    Barn Painting 165
The Egg Tree (Milhous) 166
    Complementary Color Mixing 166
The Little Island (MacDonald) 167
    Fish Under the Sea 167
    Moonlit Night 168
Many Moons (Thurber) 169
    Castle Painting 169
Song of the Swallows (Politi) 170
    Flowers 170
    Swallow Painting 171
A Tree Is Nice (Udry) 172
    Tree Painting 172
    Winter Day Painting 173
Tuesday (Wiesner) 174
    Night Scene 174
White Snow, Bright Snow (Tresselt) 175
    Houses in the Snow 175

11—PRINTS 177

Baboushka and the Three Kings (Robbins) 178
    Trees in the Snow 178
Finders Keepers (Will and Nicolas) 179
    Dog Prints 179
The Funny Little Woman (Mosel) 180
    Line Prints 180
Once a Mouse (Brown) 181
    Animal Print 181
    Crayon Rubbings on a Raised-Glue Surface 182
Sam, Bangs & Moonshine (Ness) 183
    Cat in the Window 183
    Lighthouse Print 184
    String Print 185
The Snowy Day (Keats) 186
    Snowflake Stamping 186
A Story A Story (Haley) 187
    Hornet Print 187
    Two-Color Figure Print 188
    Web Print 189

11—PRINTS (*continued*)

Sylvester and the Magic Pebble (Steig) 190
    Changing Seasons 190
White Snow, Bright Snow (Tresselt) 191
    Monoprint Snow Painting 191

Appendix: Caldecott Award Winners, 1938-1994 193

About the Author 199

Introduction

The Caldecott Medal, first awarded in 1938, is bestowed annually on the year's most distinguished American picture book for children.

Art Through Children's Literature uses these award-winning books as a source for classroom teachers to provide students with lessons that combine art and children's literature. The book contains three lessons for each of these 57 Caldecott books from 1938-1994. Lessons focus on key art concepts contained in the illustrations of these Caldecott books. Students have the opportunity to create artwork with qualities similar to the artwork in the books.

The book is divided into 11 methods of producing artwork. They include pencil, crayon, marker, colored pencil, chalk, stencils, collage, watercolor, tempera, color mixing, and printmaking. Lessons focus not only on methods of producing art, but also on art principles and elements such as line, color, texture, shape, space, and value—all important art basics.

The step-by-step activities are designed for teachers with little or no art training. Lessons are classroom tested and can be adapted to suit grades kindergarten through sixth.

Art Elements

Art elements are the main ingredients an artist uses when creating a work of art. The elements consist of color, value, line, shape, texture, and space. (The figures on page xiv represent these art elements in pictures.) These terms are referred to throughout this book and are ones with which you will need to be familiar. These elements are illustrated here to help serve as a guide when using this book.

Glossary of Art Elements

Line. Straight or curved, organic, geometric, contour, and interior.

Shape. Symmetrical (same on both sides), asymmetrical (different on each side), organic (made by nature), geometric (made by humans), abstract (nonrepresentational), representational (conveys how an object looks), positive (the actual shape), and negative (space around the object).

Space. Two-dimensional (measured by height and width) and three-dimensional (measured by height, width, and depth).

Value. Lightness or darkness of a color.

Texture. The surface quality of an object

Line

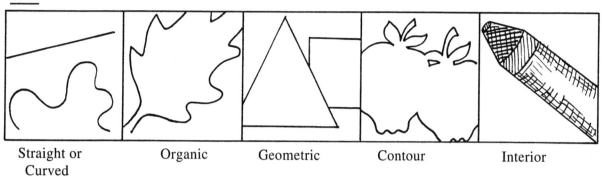

| Straight or Curved | Organic | Geometric | Contour | Interior |

Shape

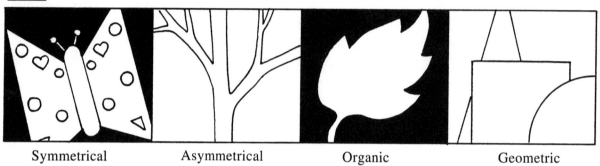

| Symmetrical | Asymmetrical | Organic | Geometric |

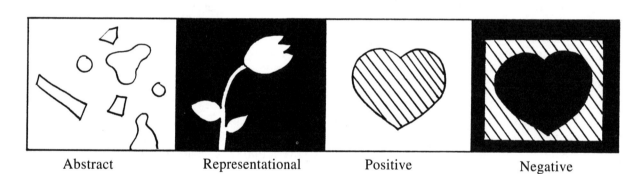

| Abstract | Representational | Positive | Negative |

Space   Value   Texture

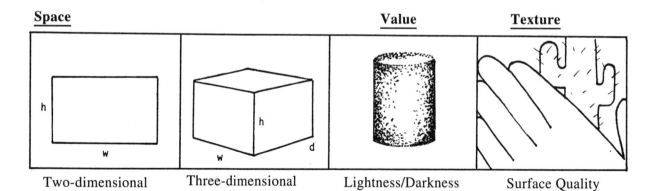

| Two-dimensional | Three-dimensional | Lightness/Darkness | Surface Quality |

The art elements of line, shape, space, value, and texture.

The Color Wheel

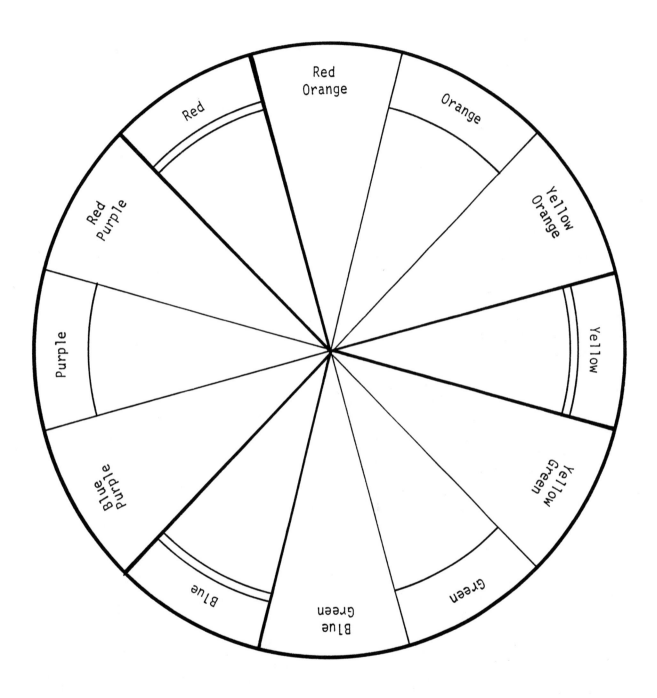

Color Wheel

Hue. The name of a color

Primary. Red, blue, and yellow

Secondary. Orange, green, and purple

Intermediate. Red orange, yellow orange, yellow green, blue green, blue purple, and red purple

Intensity. Brightness or dullness of a color

Cool colors. Green, blue, and purple—colors that recede

Warm colors. Red, yellow, and orange—colors that advance

Monochromatic color. Color with white or black

Analogous. Three colors side by side on the color wheel

Complementary. Opposites on the color wheel

Neutrals. White, gray, and black

Value. Lightness or darkness of a color

Shade. Color with black

Tint. Color with white

From *Art Through Children's Literature*. ©1994. Teacher Ideas Press, P.O. Box 6633, Englewood, CO 80155-6633, 1-800-237-6124.

Chapter
1

The lessons in this chapter focus on using pencil as the main drawing tool. Lessons explore the use of lines to achieve a variety of effects. They include simple line drawings, repetition of lines, and using line to give objects three-dimensional form. Materials required to complete the lessons are minimal: a standard #2 school pencil and any type of paper such as white drawing paper, manila paper, or photocopy paper may be used.

Abraham Lincoln
By Ingri and Edgar Parin d'Aulaire
(New York: Doubleday, 1939)
1940 Caldecott Award Winner

The story of a great president from his boyhood on the edge of the
wilderness to the Civil War and the Emancipation Proclamation.

Log Cabin

Examine the individual logs in the illustration of the log cabin. Shading is used to give the flat shapes
form. Students can draw the logs of a cabin and use shading to give the appearance of form.

Art Concept: Shape Versus Form. Shapes are two-dimensional and are measured by height and
width. Forms are three-dimensional and are measured by height, width, and depth.

Materials. Paper
Pencils

Instructions.

1. Demonstrate for the class how to
   draw a log. With a pencil, draw two
   parallel lines with a small space in
   between. Draw a curved line on
   each end.

2. Use small pencil strokes to shade
   the edges of the log but leave the
   center of the log white.

3. Instruct the students to use a pencil
   to build a house one log at a time.
   Leave open spaces for the windows
   and doors. They should shade the
   logs to complete the drawing after
   building the cabin.

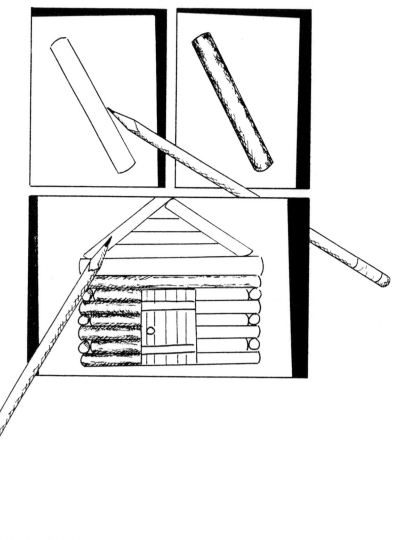

Ashanti to Zulu: African Traditions
Illustrated by Leo and Diane Dillon
Written by Margaret Musgrove
(New York: Dial, 1976)
1977 Caldecott Award Winner

Traditions and customs of various African peoples are explored
in paragraphs which begin with letters from A to Z.

Contour Line Trees

Artists use lines to define the edges of shapes in their drawings. Have students draw a tree or group of flowers using this technique.

Art Concept: Contour Lines. Used to define the edge of a shape

Materials. Paper
Pencils

Instructions.
1. Review the different tree and flower shapes found in the book's artwork, noting especially the various shapes of trunks and leaves. Ask the students to draw a tree or group of flowers using contour lines, but instruct them not to color in the shapes.

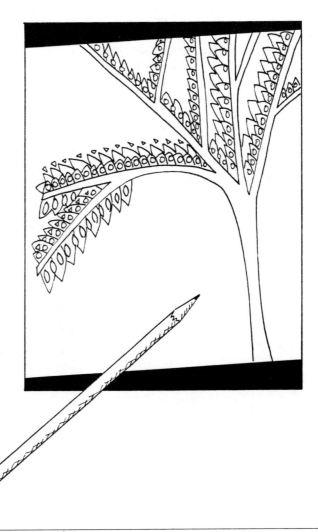

Baboushka and the Three Kings
Illustrated by Nicolas Sidjakov
Written by Ruth Robbins
(Berkeley, Calif.: Parnassus, 1960)
1961 Caldecott Award Winner

A Russian legend about a woman and her search for the Christ child.

Village

Repeated lines are used to illustrate the buildings in the village drawings. Students can draw their own villages using repeating lines.

Art Concept: Line. Repeated to make a design

Materials. Paper
Pencils
Rulers if desired

Instructions.
1. Instruct the students to use a pencil to lightly draw a square or rectangle.

2. Have them draw vertical or horizontal lines side by side inside of the geometric shape.

3. Have them repeat with additional geometric shapes and lines to create a village.

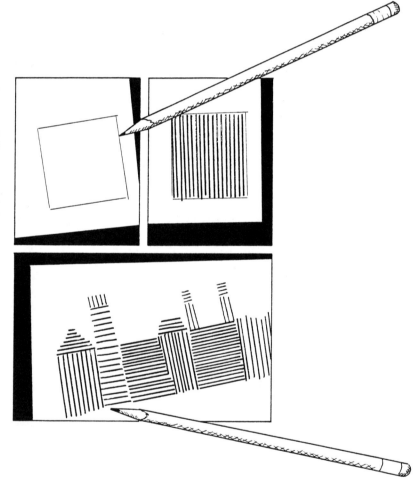

From *Art Through Children's Literature*. ©1994. Teacher Ideas Press, P.O. Box 6633, Englewood, CO 80155-6633, 1-800-237-6124.

The Big Snow
By Berta and Elmer Hader
(New York: Macmillan, 1948)
1949 Caldecott Award Winner

Animals prepare for the winter snow.

Drawing with an Eraser

Examine the leaves in the illustration as the robin holds the worm in his mouth. Notice that the leaves near the top have white veins in the center. Students can achieve a similar look by using an eraser as a drawing tool.

<u>**Art Concept: Eraser**</u>. Can be used as a drawing tool

<u>**Materials**</u>.　White paper
　　　　　　　　Leaves for tracing
　　　　　　　　Pencils
　　　　　　　　Erasers
　　　　　　　　Scrap paper
　　　　　　　　Cotton swabs

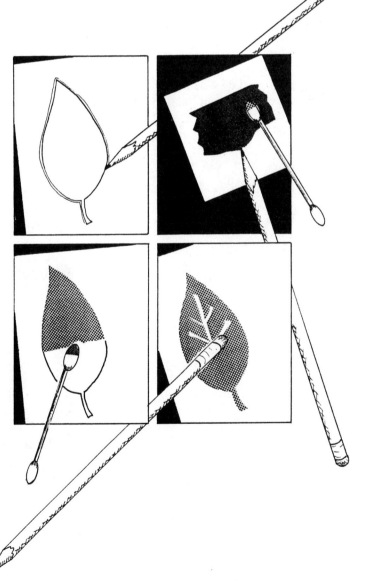

<u>**Instructions**</u>.

1.　Provide students with several leaves and ask them to trace their shapes onto the drawing paper with a pencil.

2.　On a piece of scrap paper, have the students scribble with a pencil in one area to build up graphite from the pencil. Then rub the end of a cotton swab across the graphite.

3.　Fill in the leaf shape with the graphite from the swab.

4.　To make the veins, have them use an eraser as an additional drawing tool.

Black and White
By David Macaulay
(Boston: Houghton Mifflin, 1990)
1991 Caldecott Award Winner

Words and pictures tell four stories at one time about a train, cows, commuters, and parents.

Subtle Changes

Notice the illustrations in the story "A Waiting Game." The artist repeats the same building in the illustrations. The changes from one picture to the next are subtle. Using pencil, students can make an illustration which shows a sequence of events with subtle changes.

Art Concept: Progressive Drawing. Step-by-step changes in a drawing

Materials.   Paper
Pencils

Instructions.

1. Instruct the students to divide their papers into four sections. Using a pencil, draw the same building in each space.

2. Have them add subtle changes to each drawing.

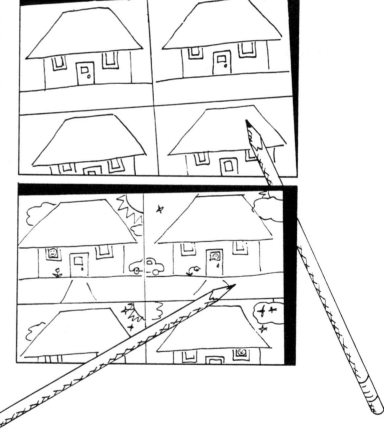

From *Art Through Children's Literature*. ©1994. Teacher Ideas Press, P.O. Box 6633, Englewood, CO 80155-6633, 1-800-237-6124.

Hey, Al
Illustrated by Richard Egielski
Written by Arthur Yorinks
(New York: Farrar, 1986)
1987 Caldecott Award Winner

A janitor and his dog leave their boring lives to live in what appears to be paradise.

Bird Drawing

When Al begins to turn into a bird, part of his body is human and part is a bird's body. Ask the class to draw themselves turning into a bird and to combine the two types of organic shapes.

Art Concept: Organic Shapes. Made by nature

Materials.　　Paper
　　　　　　　Pencils

Instructions.

1. Show the class the different types of birds illustrated throughout the book. Examine the different-shaped legs, beaks, feathers, and bodies. Have the students draw a picture with a pencil of how they would look changing into a bird.

Hey, Al

Illustrated by Richard Egielski
Written by Arthur Yorinks
(New York: Farrar, 1986)
1987 Caldecott Award Winner

A janitor and his dog leave their boring lives to live in what appears to be paradise.

Boxed Room

The artist places Al's room in a boxed area. The space beyond is indicated by placing a few objects on and outside of the box. Using this technique, students can make their own drawings of a room.

Art Concept: Implied Space. Image continues beyond what is seen

Materials.   Paper
Pencils

Instructions.
1. Instruct the students to draw a rectangle on their paper.

2. Have them draw a smaller rectangle inside the first rectangle.

3. Have them connect the corners of the two shapes.

4. Students can add furniture to the room, and details may be added to the outside of the box to show that the space continues.

Madeline's Rescue
By Ludwig Bemelmans
(New York: Viking, 1953)
1954 Caldecott Award Winner

Madeline is rescued from drowning by a dog.

Architectural Landmarks

Throughout the book the artist shows many architectural landmarks found in Paris. They serve as backdrops and are important elements in the story. Madeline, for example, falls from the Pont Neuf Bridge—a very old and famous bridge. Other landmarks such as the Institute of France appear on the book's cover, and the girls search for Genevieve in Tuileries, a park. Using an architectural landmark with which they are familiar, the students can draw Madeline and the girls on their search for Genevieve.

Art Concept: Architecture. The art of building

Materials.   Paper
               Pencils

Instructions.
1. Discuss with the students the landmarks—listed on the inside of the book jacket—that are shown in the story. Talk about landmarks that the students are familiar with in their city, state, or country. Ask them to select one and draw it, being sure to include Madeline and the girls as they search for Genevieve.

Madeline's Rescue
By Ludwig Bemelmans
(New York: Viking, 1953)
1954 Caldecott Award Winner

Madeline is rescued from drowning by a dog.

Faces

Look at the illustrations of Madeline and the girls in the story, noting the simple but expressive lines the artist uses in drawing the girls. Using minimal lines, students can draw faces that show a variety of emotions.

Art Concept: Line. Has expressive qualities

Materials.   Paper
Pencils

Instructions.

1. Have students draw four circles on their paper.

2. Select students to demonstrate the position of the face when feeling sadness, anger, fear, and happiness. Under each circle ask the students to write the emotion they are going to draw, then draw features on the circles to illustrate these emotions. Have them complete the drawings by adding hair and hats to the faces.

May I Bring a Friend?
Illustrated by Beni Montresor
Written by Beatrice Schenk de Regniers
(New York: Atheneum, 1964)
1965 Caldecott Award Winner

A young boy is invited to visit the king and queen, and brings along his friends from the zoo.

Doorways

Examine the illustration of the king and queen greeting their guest and the monkeys. By placing one doorway inside of another and progressively making them smaller, the artist illustrates the vastness of the king and queen's home. The floor's pattern decreases in size to indicate depth, a technique students can imitate by making a drawing of doorways.

Art Concept: Depth. Objects that diminish in size

Materials. Paper
Pencils

Instructions.

1. Instruct the students to use a pencil to draw the shape of a doorway. Add the lines that show where the wall and the floor meet.

2. Have them draw a smaller doorway inside of the first, a smaller doorway inside of the second, and so on.

3. Have students draw a pattern on the floor that decreases in size as it goes through the doorways. The students may add animals to the drawing if they wish.

Mei Li

By Thomas Handforth
(New York: Doubleday, 1938)
1939 Caldecott Award Winner

A story about a little girl and her visit to the New Year's Day Fair.

Neighborhood Map

The artist uses a map to show the locations where the story takes place. Details are used in the illustration. Using such details, the students may make their own map that shows their route to school.

Art Concept: Details. Small parts of a large image

Materials.   Paper
Pencils

Instructions.

1.   Instruct the students to draw the places surrounding their home and school. Direct them to use details, such as a flag on a schoolhouse, and add labels to describe the various locations.

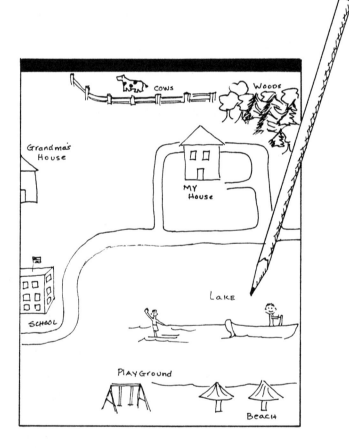

They Were Strong and Good
By Robert Lawson
(New York: Viking, 1940)
1941 Caldecott Award Winner

A story about the author's ancestors and how they helped build America.

Sky and Tree Drawings

The illustration of the hunt shows how different types of lines are used to represent the trees. Using this method students can draw a landscape.

Art Concept: Variety of Lines. Used to indicate different types of objects

Materials.   Drawing paper
Pencils

Instructions.

1. Direct the students to draw a picture of a landscape using a variety of pencil lines to indicate objects such as trees, grass, clouds, and hills.

From *Art Through Children's Literature*. ©1994. Teacher Ideas Press, P.O. Box 6633, Englewood, CO 80155-6633, 1-800-237-6124.

They Were Strong and Good
By Robert Lawson
(New York: Viking, 1940)
1941 Caldecott Award Winner

A story about the author's ancestors and how they helped build America.

Sky with Value Changes

The sky above the father as he walks back to Alabama shows variations in value. Small lines grouped together form the clouds in the sky. Students can use this method to draw a sky.

Art Concept: Value. Light and dark areas can be achieved by the placement of lines in a drawing

Materials.　Paper
　　　　　　　Pencils

Instructions.

1.　Ask the students to draw a picture of the sky with clouds by using a variety of pencil strokes. Students can make dark areas by placing lines close together; lines placed farther apart create light areas.

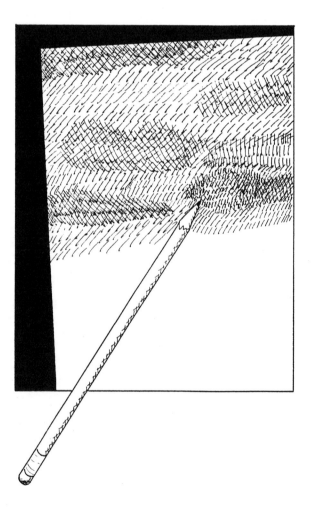

Tuesday
By David Wiesner
(New York: Clarion Books, 1991)
1992 Caldecott Award Winner

Frogs rise on their lily pads, float through the air, and explore
the nearby houses while the inhabitants sleep.

Drawing Frogs

The main subjects in the story are frogs, which the artist draws in a variety of sizes, shapes, and views. Students can learn to draw frogs by using simple shapes.

Art Concept: Shape. Students may draw the body of a frog by simplifying its form into basic shapes

Materials. Paper
Pencils

Instructions.

1. Demonstrate for the students how to draw a frog by first drawing a circle.

2. Draw two circles on top for eyes. Add two smaller circles inside of the larger circles.

3. On the left side of the circle draw a *c* for a leg. On the right side, draw a backward *c* for the other leg. Then draw the frog's mouth.

4. To make the feet, connect three *v* shapes.

5. Draw the lily pad. Ask the students to imitate this method to draw frogs of their own.

Chapter
2

Wax crayons are available in a range of colors and sizes. Most often they are used for drawing lines or coloring in areas using the pointed end. This chapter explores this traditional use of crayons as well as nontraditional uses. Nontraditional uses include drawing with the side of a peeled crayon and crayon rubbings.

Animals of the Bible, A Picture Book
Illustrated by Dorothy P. Lathrop
Text selected by Helen Dean Fish
(New York: Lippencott, 1937)
1938 Caldecott Award Winner

These animal stories are derived from the King James version of the Old and New Testaments.

Leaf Drawing with Contrast

The dark background in the illustration of Balaam contrasts with the leaves in the foreground. Using a black crayon, the students may make a leaf drawing that shows contrast.

Art Concept: Contrast. Light versus dark

Materials.   Paper
Black crayons

Instructions.

1. Instruct the students to draw the shape of leaves and stems on their paper using a black crayon. Have them color the background black to show the contrast. The crayon should be applied heavily so that the paper does not show through.

Animals of the Bible, A Picture Book
Illustrated by Dorothy P. Lathrop
Text selected by Helen Dean Fish
(New York: Lippencott, 1937)
1938 Caldecott Award Winner

These animal stories are derived from the King James version of the Old and New Testaments.

Leaf Rubbing
Notice the contrast of the leaves in the drawing of the hen and her chicks. The students can make a similar drawing of leaves with contrast by using a rubbing method.

Art Concept: Contrast. Light versus dark

Materials.   Black crayons
Assortment of leaves
White photocopy
      paper
Newspaper

Instructions.

1. Lay a leaf back side up on a piece of newspaper. Instruct the students to rub over the back surface of the leaf using the side of a peeled black crayon.

2. Have them place the leaf under the white paper and rub the paper with the side of a pencil to transfer the crayon. Return the leaf to the newspaper, apply more crayon, and repeat the rubbing process. The same leaf or a new one can be used.

3. Have them color in the area behind the leaves using the black crayon.

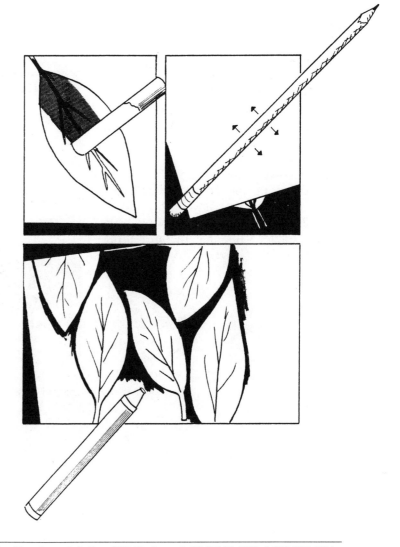

Animals of the Bible, A Picture Book
Illustrated by Dorothy P. Lathrop
Text selected by Helen Dean Fish
(New York: Lippencott, 1937)
1938 Caldecott Award Winner

These animal stories are derived from the King James version of the Old and New Testaments.

Value Sky Drawing

Look at the sky behind the animals in the illustration of the story of Noah. Notice how the value changes from light to dark. Using crayon the students can make a picture of the sky showing a value change.

Art Concept: Value. Degree of light and dark

Materials.   Paper
Pencils
Crayons

Instructions.

1. Ask the students to begin by drawing the shape of hills with a pencil. Next instruct them to color at the top of the paper by pressing hard with the crayon.

2. As students continue coloring down the paper they should decrease the pressure on the crayon. The area near the hills should have a lighter value than the area at the top of the paper.

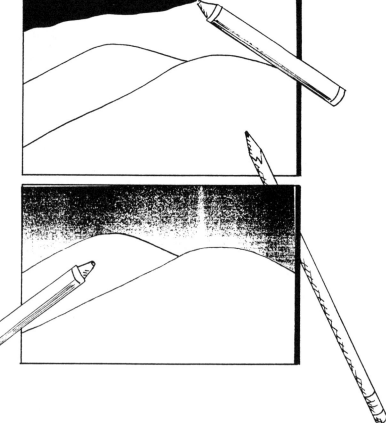

Cinderella, or the Little Glass Slipper
Illustrated and translated by Marcia Brown
Written by Charles Perrault
(New York: Scribner, 1954)
1955 Caldecott Award Winner

A romantic tale about a young girl, her stepfamily, and a prince.

Coach Design

Cinderella's godmother transforms a pumpkin into a coach whose shape is similar to the pumpkin's. Imagine the possibilities if Cinderella had brought a different item from the garden—perhaps a radish or a carrot. Using a pencil and a crayon students can stylize their own version of a coach.

Art Concept: Stylize. Artists change the usual look of an object to fit their own idea of how something should look

Materials. Paper
Pencils
Crayons

Instructions.
1. Instruct the students to begin by drawing the basic shape of a fruit or vegetable using a pencil.

2. Then have them transform the shape into a coach with a crayon and pencil.

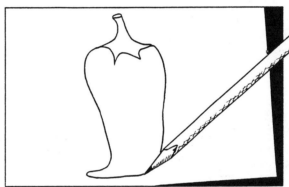

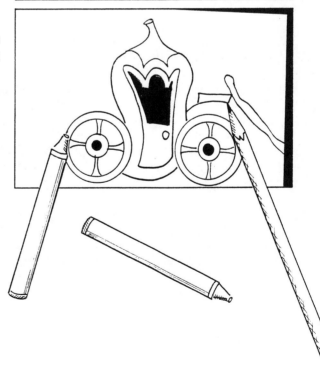

Drummer Hoff
Illustrated by Ed Emberley
Written by Barbara Emberley
(Englewood Cliffs, N.J.: Prentice-Hall, 1967)
1968 Caldecott Award Winner

A story told in verse about the assembling and firing of a cannon.

Kahbahbloom Drawing

The colors used to show the explosion are bold and expressive. The black outline contributes to the colors' strong quality. Students can create their own explosive design with crayon.

Art Concept: Color. Bright colors can be used as an expressive element

Materials.   Colored construction
paper
Crayons

Instructions.

1. Provide a variety of colored construction paper for students to select from. Instruct the students to begin the drawing with a simple shape drawn heavily with black crayon.

2. They should continue to build around that shape with additional shapes. Remind the students to press down with the crayon. The black will not appear as bold if the colored construction paper is visible through the crayon. Students should color the shapes after all the lines have been drawn.

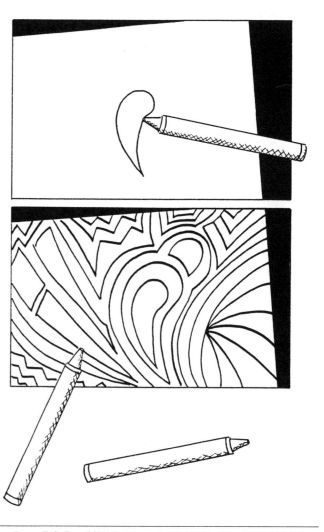

Drummer Hoff
Illustrated by Ed Emberley
Written by Barbara Emberley
(Englewood Cliffs, N.J.: Prentice-Hall, 1967)
1968 Caldecott Award Winner

A story told in verse about the assembling and firing of a cannon.

Uniforms with Patterns

Notice the uniforms that the soldiers are wearing in the story. The uniforms are divided into smaller areas that create patterns. Students can make their own characters with patterned clothing.

Art Concept: Pattern. Repetition of a line or shape

Materials. Paper
Pencils
Crayons

Instructions.

1. Have students use a pencil to draw a soldier.

2. Then have them divide the soldier's uniform into small areas with patterns and add color with crayons.

Duffy and the Devil
Illustrated by Margot Zemach
Retold by Harve Zemach
(New York: Farrar, 1973)
1974 Caldecott Award Winner

A variation of the story of Rumpelstiltskin with an unusual ending.

Witches Gathering

As Squire Lovel enters the cavern he sees witches at its rear. Notice how the technique of size that the artist uses to illustrate these witches gives the appearance of depth to the illustration. Students can use this method to draw witches.

Art Concept: Size. Large objects appear close to the viewer, and smaller objects appear farther away

Materials. Paper
Pencils
Crayons

Instructions.
1. Instruct the students to use size as a key element in drawing a group of witches as they would look dancing around a fire. The students should draw with the pencil first, then add color with crayons.

Fables
By Arnold Lobel
(New York: Harper & Row, 1980)
1981 Caldecott Award Winner

Twenty fables about an array of animal characters from
crocodile to ostrich, each containing a clever moral.

Seashore

The illustration of the mouse sitting on the rock at the seashore is an example of zones. Space is represented through the use of a foreground, middle ground, and a background. Students can make a landscape drawing with zones.

Art Concept: Zones. The foreground, middle ground, and background

Materials. Paper
Pencils
Crayons

Instructions.

1. Ask the students to begin by drawing shapes in the three zones. Objects such as rocks and sand should be in the foreground. Students may draw the water in the middle ground and the sky and sun in the background. Have them complete the drawing by adding color with crayons.

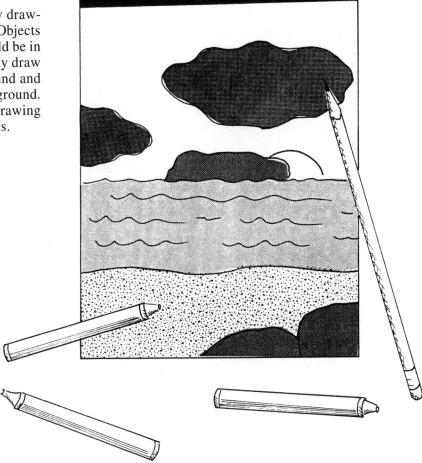

From *Art Through Children's Literature*. ©1994. Teacher Ideas Press, P.O. Box 6633, Englewood, CO 80155-6633, 1-800-237-6124.

The Fool of the World and the Flying Ship
Illustrated by Uri Shulevitz
Retold by Arthur Ransome
(New York: Farrar, 1968)
1969 Caldecott Award Winner

When the Czar proclaims that he will marry his daughter to the man who brings
him a flying ship, the Fool of the World sets out to try his luck and meets
some unusual companions along the way.

Palace Drawing

Notice the palace's dome shapes—a popular element in Russian architecture. Students can make a drawing of the czar's palace using dome shapes.

Art Concept: Russian Architecture. The dome is a common element

Materials.   Paper
Pencils
Crayons

Instructions.

1. Discuss the differences between the buildings that they see on a daily basis and the Czar's palace. Ask them to draw with a pencil their own version of a Russian palace. Then have them use crayons to add color.

Frog Went A-Courtin'
Illustrated by Feodor Rojankovsky
Retold by John Langstaff
(New York: Harcourt, Brace, 1955)
1956 Caldecott Award Winner

A story based upon a song about the wedding of a frog and a mouse.

Wedding Guest
To illustrate the size of the wedding guests in the story and to give the viewer a sense of scale, the artist places large objects near the guests. Notice, for example, the size of the flea compared to that of the leaf. Using this method the students can draw a wedding guest.

Art Concept: Scale. Size of an object

Materials.　Paper
　　　　　　Pencils
　　　　　　Crayons

Instructions.
1.　Ask the students to use a pencil to draw one of the wedding guests. To show the guest's size, place items such as grass and leaves, near the guest. Have students add color with crayons.

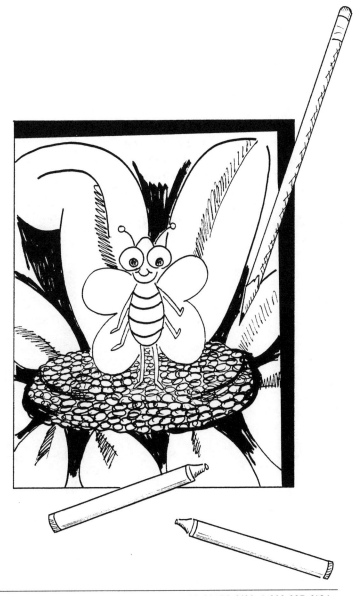

The Funny Little Woman
Illustrated by Blair Lent
Retold by Arlene Mosel
(New York: Dutton, 1972)
1973 Caldecott Award Winner

A Japanese woman follows a rice dumpling into a hole in the ground
where she encounters a wicked Oni.

Two Worlds

The artist shows two worlds in the illustrations: the world above and the world below ground. Color is used in the area in which the funny little woman is located. Using this method the students can illustrate their own idea of the two worlds and the wicked Oni.

Art Concept: Color. Used to emphasize one area of a picture

Materials. Paper
Pencils
Crayons

Instructions.

1. Instruct students to divide the paper into two sections—above and below ground. Using a pencil the students may draw the two worlds, adding their own version of Oni and the funny little woman. The students should then select which area they want the viewer to look at first and add color to that area.

The Girl Who Loved Wild Horses
By Paul Goble
(New York: Bradbury Press, 1978)
1979 Caldecott Award Winner

Although she is fond of her people, a young girl prefers living among
wild horses where she is truly happy and free.

Geometric Blankets

The blanket designs throughout the book are painted with the colors red, blue, white, and black. The shapes used are geometric. The combination of the shapes and colors create a balanced, symmetrical design. Students may design a symmetrical Native American blanket using similar colors and shapes.

<u>Art Concept: Balance</u>. The placement of the colors and shapes in a symmetrical design

<u>Materials</u>.
- Large drawing paper
- Pencils
- Crayons
- Rulers
- Coins

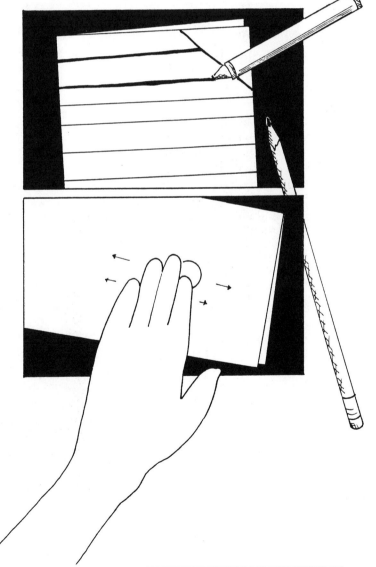

<u>Instructions</u>.

1. Direct the students to fold the drawing paper in half. On half of the paper begin drawing the blanket design using a pencil. Use squares, triangles, and stripes for the design. Make sure that the center of the blanket is on the fold. Pressing hard, trace over the lines with black crayon.

2. To transfer the lines, fold the paper inside out so that the crayon lines are on the inside of the folded paper. With a coin placed flat on the paper, rub the back surface of the crayon drawing. This transfers the lines to the opposite side of the paper.

3. The lines will be very light, making it necessary to go over the tops of them with black crayon.

---

4. Using crayons, add color to the
   blanket. Remind the students that
   the blanket design is symmetrical
   and that the same color should be
   on both sides of the drawing.

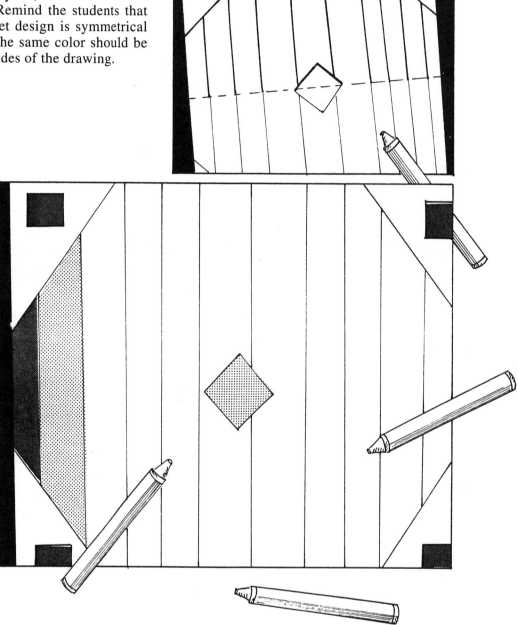

The Girl Who Loved Wild Horses
By Paul Goble
(New York: Bradbury Press, 1978)
1979 Caldecott Award Winner

Although she is fond of her people, a young girl prefers living among
wild horses where she is truly happy and free.

Symmetrical Sun Design

A circle and triangles are the shapes used in the sun design at the end of the story. The design is symmetrical—identical on both sides. Using the technique described below, the students can make a symmetrical sun design.

<u>Art Concept: **Symmetry**</u>. Balanced on both sides of a center axis

<u>Materials</u>.   Large drawing paper
Pencils
Crayons
Rulers
Coins

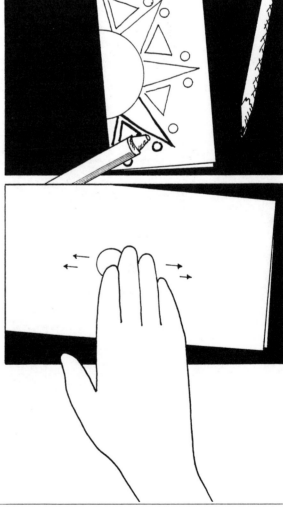

<u>Instructions</u>.

1. Direct the students to fold a large sheet of paper in half. On half of the paper draw with a pencil a half of a sun, ensuring that the center of the sun is on the fold. Trace over the lines with black crayon, pressing hard.

2. Fold the paper inside out so that the crayon lines are on the inside of the paper. With a coin placed flat on the paper, rub the back surface of the crayon drawing. This transfers the lines to the opposite side of the paper.

---

3. The lines will be light, so it will be necessary to retrace them with black crayon.

4. Students can add color to the sun with crayons. Remind them, however, that the sun design is symmetrical and that the same color should be on both sides of the drawing.

The Glorious Flight:
Across the Channel with Louis Blériot
By Alice and Martin Provensen
(New York: Viking, 1983)
1984 Caldecott Award Winner

A biography of the man whose fascination with flying machines produced the Blériot XI, which crossed the English Channel in thirty-seven minutes in the early 1900s.

Buildings in the City of Cambrai
Notice the side streets in the illustrations of the city. The size of the buildings diminish to show their distance from the viewer. Using this method of decreasing size, students can make a drawing of the town of Cambrai.

Art Concept: Diminishing Size. Used to create the illusion of depth

Materials. Paper
Pencils
Crayons
Rulers

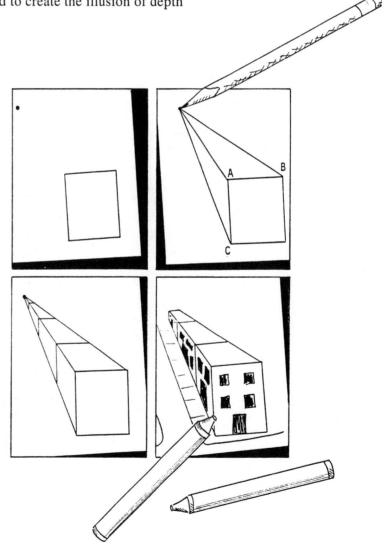

Instructions.
1. With a pencil, have students draw a rectangular shape near the bottom of the paper placed to the right of center. Draw a dot in the upper-left corner.

2. Using a ruler, draw three lines from corners A, B, and C to the dot.

3. Draw lines vertically and horizontally to show the individual buildings.

4.   Add details such as windows, doors, and the road. Add color with crayons.

Grandfather's Journey
By Allen Say
(Boston: Houghton Mifflin, 1993)
1994 Caldecott Award Winner

A Japanese American man recounts his grandfather's journey to America, which he later also undertakes, and the feelings of being torn by a love for two different countries.

Portrait

The artist begins and ends the story with portraits of his grandfather. Notice that a variety of shades of brown are used to convey the idea that the portraits are from a long time ago. Using brown crayon over the top of a photocopy, students may make their own portraits appear older.

Art Concept: Monochromatic. Light and dark shades of a single color

Materials.   Photocopy of student
                        photographs
              Brown crayons

Instructions.
1. Ask the students to bring photographs of themselves to school—preferably portrait style. Make photocopies of each picture. Instruct the students to color over the top of the image with brown crayon, applying it heavily over dark areas and lightly over the white areas.

Hey, Al
Illustrated by Richard Egielski
Written by Arthur Yorinks
(New York: Farrar, 1986)
1987 Caldecott Award Winner

A janitor and his dog leave their boring lives to live in what appears to be paradise.

Paradise Drawing

Different color schemes are used to illustrate the difference between the island and Al's room. Using bright colors students can draw their own idea of the island.

Art Concept: Color. Used as an expressive element

Materials. Paper
Pencils
Crayons

Instructions.

1. Ask the students to draw, with a pencil, their idea of paradise. Use crayons to add color to the island drawing.

The Little House
By Virginia Lee Burton
(Boston: Houghton Mifflin, 1942)
1943 Caldecott Award Winner

A story about a little house and the changes that occur because of progress.

Landscape Drawing

To show depth the artist uses size as a key element. The trees in the background, for example, are smaller than those in the foreground. The students may make their own landscape drawing that shows depth.

Art Concept: Depth. Created through the use of different size objects

Materials. Paper
Pencils
Crayons

Instructions.

1. Direct the students to begin by drawing the little house on their paper. Add trees to the drawing, decreasing the size of the trees to show depth. They can add color with crayons.

The Little House
By Virginia Lee Burton
(Boston: Houghton Mifflin, 1942)
1943 Caldecott Award Winner

A story about a little house and the changes that occur because of progress.

Little House at Night

Notice the illustration of the little house at the end of the story. The evening sky is made up of small strokes of color. Students can imitate this method using crayons to make a drawing of a little house at night.

Art Concept: Crayon. Can be used to make a drawing with obvious strokes

Materials.   Paper
Pencils
Crayons

Instructions.
1. Have students begin by drawing the shape of a house with a pencil. Add other items such as trees and stars, then add color with a crayon. Use small strokes to color the sky around the little house.

The Little House
By Virginia Lee Burton
(Boston: Houghton Mifflin, 1942)
1943 Caldecott Award Winner

A story about a little house and the changes that occur because of progress.

Seasons

The artist uses color to illustrate the little house during the changing seasons . Students may make a drawing that shows the little house and how it would look at different times of the year.

Art Concept: Color. Used as an expressive element

Materials.   Paper
Pencils
Crayons

Instructions.

1. Have students divide a sheet of paper into four sections. With a pencil draw the little house in each section of the paper. Color the sections using colors and shapes to show the season. Remind the students that certain objects, like trees, will change during the different seasons.

Make Way for Ducklings
By Robert McCloskey
(New York: Viking, 1941)
1942 Caldecott Award Winner

A story of a mother duck and her ducklings' journey through Boston.

Buildings

Notice the buildings at the end of the story as night falls and the ducklings return to the little island. The buildings have a three-dimensional look. Using a peeled brown crayon laid on its side, students can make a drawing of such three-dimensional buildings.

Art Concepts:

Crayon. By applying varied pressure to a crayon, marks can be made that give form to a shape

Form. Measured by height, width, and depth

Materials.
Paper
Brown crayons

Instructions.

1. Have students begin by drawing the front of the building. Lay the crayon straight across the paper, and pull the crayon down.

2. To make the front of the building wider, lay the crayon next to the first stroke and repeat.

3. To make the side of the building, turn the crayon at an angle and make a stroke. Repeat the above steps to make additional buildings. Make a line across the bottom for the ground, and add doors and windows.

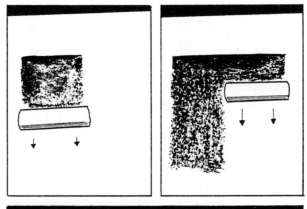

From *Art Through Children's Literature*. ©1994. Teacher Ideas Press, P.O. Box 6633, Englewood, CO 80155-6633, 1-800-237-6124.

Make Way for Ducklings
By Robert McCloskey
(New York: Viking, 1941)
1942 Caldecott Award Winner

A story of a mother duck and her ducklings' journey through Boston.

Duck Drawing

Lines are used to show the texture of the ducklings' feathers. Using crayon, students can make a drawing of a duckling.

Art Concept: Texture. Surface quality of an object

Materials. Paper
Pencils
Brown crayons

Instructions.

1. Demonstrate for the class how to draw a duck. Begin with an oval shape drawn with pencil.

2. Then draw a smaller oval for the head. Add the shape of a bill and an eye.

3. Connect the two ovals with a neck. Using a brown crayon add small lines to show the texture of the feathers.

Make Way for Ducklings
By Robert McCloskey
(New York: Viking, 1941)
1942 Caldecott Award Winner

A story of a mother duck and her ducklings' journey through Boston.

Island Drawing

Using the side of a peeled crayon, students may make a drawing of the island where the ducklings live.

Art Concept: Crayon. A peeled crayon may be used to make a wider mark on a paper

Materials.   Paper
Pencils
Brown crayons

Instructions.

1. Provide the students with a brown crayon from which the paper has been peeled. Lay the crayon on its side and draw a small, curved shape for the island. Vary the pressure on the crayon.

2. Draw tree trunks by again laying the crayon on its side and making long strokes. To make the smaller branches, turn the crayon at an angle and make shorter strokes.

3. Add leaves by moving the crayon in a circular motion. Finish the drawing by adding water and grass.

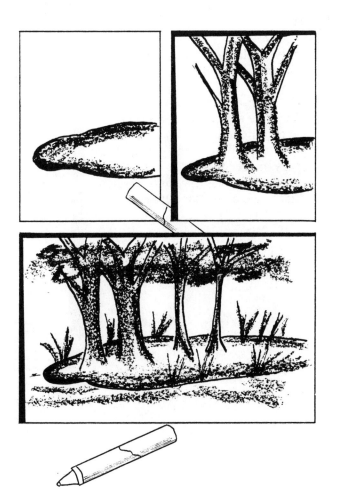

May I Bring a Friend?
Illustrated by Beni Montresor
Written by Beatrice Schenk de Regniers
(New York: Atheneum, 1964)
1965 Caldecott Award Winner

A young boy is invited to visit the king and queen, and brings along his friends from the zoo.

Castle

The placement of the castle at the top of the story's first illustrations indicates that the castle is in the distance. Students can use this method to make a drawing of a castle.

Art Concept: Space. Achieved by placing objects meant to be in the distance higher on the paper

Materials. Pencils
Paper
Crayons

Instructions.

1. Have students use a pencil to draw a small castle near the top of their paper.

2. To draw the castle steps, begin by sketching lines across the paper that get progressively longer as they move down the page. Draw vertical lines at the ends of these lines, and add color with crayons.

Mei Li
By Thomas Handforth
(New York: Doubleday, 1938)
1939 Caldecott Award Winner

A story about a little girl and her visit to the New Year's Day Fair.

Dragon Hills

Texture can be created by placing a piece of paper on a rough surface, such as a sheet of sandpaper or a concrete sidewalk, and drawing on the paper with a crayon. Using this method students can make a drawing of dragon hills.

Art Concept: Texture. The rough surface of a piece of sandpaper or a sidewalk can be transferred to a paper by placing the paper on top of the surface and drawing with a crayon.

Materials.   Rough surface such as
       sidewalk or
       sandpaper
  Paper
  Pencils
  Black crayons

Instructions.

1. Have students lightly draw with a pencil several hill shapes on a sheet of drawing paper. Next draw the head of a dragon on top of one of the hills.

2. Instruct the students to place the pencil drawing on the top of a rough surface. Using a black crayon, color over the pencil sketch.

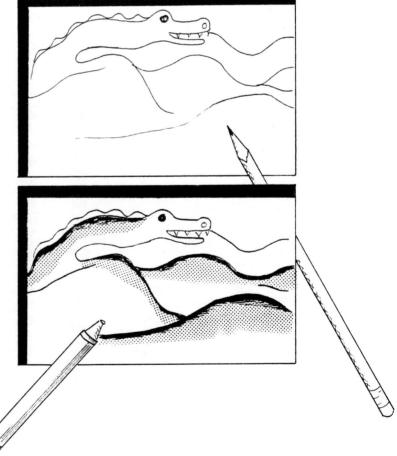

Nine Days to Christmas
Illustrated by Marie Hall Ets
Written by Marie Hall Ets and Aurora Labastida
(New York: Viking, 1959)
1960 Caldecott Award Winner

A Mexican girl named Ceci chooses a special pinata for the Christmas celebration.

Pinata at Night

Throughout the book the artist uses a limited amount of color on the gray background. The viewer's eye is attracted first to those areas with the brighter colors. Using pencil on gray paper, students may draw a picture of a pinata hanging in the night sky. Color can be added with crayons to those areas that students want the viewers to see first.

Art Concept: Emphasis. Used to direct the viewer's eye to an area

Materials.　Gray paper
　　　　　　　Pencils
　　　　　　　Crayons

Instructions.
1.　Have students draw, with a pencil, a pinata hanging from two trees. With crayons add color to the areas that students would like viewers to look at first.

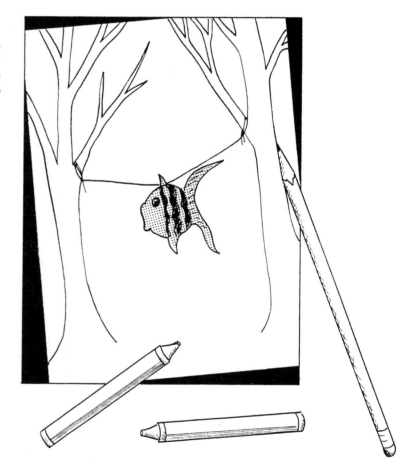

One Fine Day
Illustrated and retold by Nonny Hogrogian
(New York: Macmillan, 1971)
1972 Caldecott Award Winner

When a fox steals milk from a woman, she cuts off his tail to punish him.
He must return the milk before she will sew it back on.

Sunset Drawing

Look at the illustration of the fox as his tail is being sewn back on. The landscape is an example of zones. The small red flowers and the dark grass are in the foreground, and the trees, gold flowers, and the light grass are in the middle ground. In the background is the setting sun. Using crayons students may make a landscape drawing with zones.

Art Concept: Zones. Foreground, middle ground, and background

Materials. Paper
Pencils
Crayons

Instructions.

1. Have students draw with pencil a picture of a sunset with three zones. Place grass and flowers in the foreground. Next draw trees, grass, and smaller, less detailed flowers. Add the sun in the third zone, the background. Complete the drawing by adding color with crayons.

Owl Moon
Illustrated by John Schoenherr
Written by Jane Yolen
(New York: Philomel, 1987)
1988 Caldecott Award Winner

On a cold winter's night under a full moon, a father and daughter trek into
the woods to see the Great Horned Owl.

Landscape Drawing

Notice the landscape at the beginning of the story. The value changes from a dark background to a light foreground. Students may use white crayon on blue paper to create a landscape drawing with variations in value.

Art Concept: Value. The lightness or darkness of a color

Materials. Blue construction paper
Pencils
White crayons

Instructions.

1. Have students draw buildings and trees with a pencil.

2. Color the buildings' roofs with white crayon so that they appear to be snow covered.

3. Using the side of a small, white crayon from which the paper has been peeled, color the bottom section of the blue paper to give the appearance of snow. Gradually color toward the top of the paper, applying less pressure to the crayon to vary the value.

Ox-Cart Man
Illustrated by Barbara Cooney
Written by Donald Hall
(New York: Viking, 1979)
1980 Caldecott Award Winner

The story depicts the yearly cycle of life for a New England farmer
during the nineteenth century.

Town of Portsmouth

Observe the overlapping of the buildings in the illustration of Portsmouth—a technique that gives the illusion of depth to a picture. Students can use overlapping to draw their own picture of Portsmouth.

Art Concept: Overlapping Shapes.
Used to give the illusion of depth

Materials.　Paper
　　　　　　　Pencils
　　　　　　　Crayons

Instructions.

1.　Have students begin by drawing with pencil a variety of houses. Suggest that they draw the foreground shapes first, then the objects of the middle ground, then the background.

2.　Draw roads, trees, fences, hills, water, and ships. Add color to the picture with crayons.

From *Art Through Children's Literature*. ©1994. Teacher Ideas Press, P.O. Box 6633, Englewood, CO 80155-6633, 1-800-237-6124.

The Polar Express
By Chris Van Allsburg
(Boston: Houghton Mifflin, 1985)
1986 Caldecott Award Winner

A magical train ride on Christmas Eve takes a boy to the North Pole
to receive a special gift from Santa Claus

North Pole at Night

In the story's illustrations the intensity of the white windows shining out from the dark factories draws the viewer to look at those areas first. Using this technique, the students may draw how they imagine the factories at the North Pole look at night.

Art Concept: Emphasis. Through the use of color the artist directs the viewer's eyes to a certain area of the picture

Materials.   Brown construction paper
Pencils
Crayons

Instructions.

1. Have students draw the buildings first with pencil, then color the windows with white or yellow crayons.

2. To cover large areas such as the sky, peel the paper off of a blue crayon, lay it on its side, and rub the crayon on the paper. The look of smoke escaping from the factories' stacks can be illustrated using the same method with a white crayon.

3. Finally add white crayon dots to the drawing for snow.

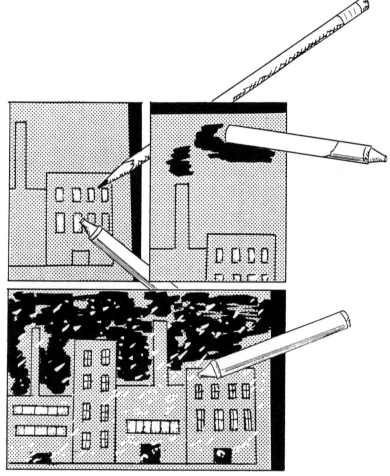

Prayer for a Child
Illustrated by Elizabeth Orton Jones
Written by Rachel Field
(New York: Macmillan, 1944)
1945 Caldecott Award Winner

This is a story about a child's bedtime prayer.

Peaceful Drawing

The words in the story express being thankful for the simple everyday things in life. The soft yellow adds to the peacefulness of the illustrations. Students may make a drawing on yellow construction paper of something for which they are thankful.

Art Concept: Color. Used as an expressive element

Materials.   Yellow construction paper
Pencils
Crayons

Instructions.

1. Ask the students to think about people and things that are special to them. Using a pencil and crayons, draw a picture of some of those special things on the yellow construction paper.

Song of the Swallows
By Leo Politi
(New York: Scribner, 1949)
1950 Caldecott Award Winner

The gardener of a church in San Juan tells a young boy a story about swallows.

Spring Garden

Pink is the dominant color that the artist uses throughout the story. It's a color choice that gives the illustrations a peaceful quality. Students may make a drawing of a spring garden using pink crayon on pink paper.

Art Concept: Color. Used to create a mood

Materials.   Pink construction paper
Pencils
Crayons

Instructions.
1.   Have students use a pencil to draw a garden. Add color to the drawing, using pink as the dominant color.

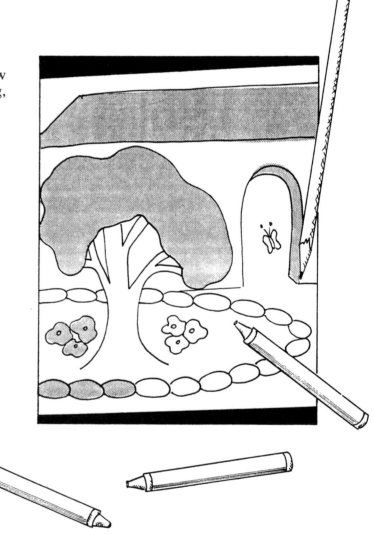

Chapter

3

Available in many colors and sizes, markers provide a more intense color than can be achieved with other drawing tools. This chapter explores the marker as a tool for line drawings, as well as a tool that may be combined with other materials such as water and crayon.

Always Room for One More
Illustrated by Nonny Hogrogian
Written by Sorche Nic Leodhas, pseud. (Leclaire Alger)
(New York: Holt, Rinehart & Winston, 1965)
1966 Caldecott Award Winner

A kind man invites passersby into his small home. Based upon the
Scottish ballad of the same title.

Figures

The artist uses lines drawn side by side and crosshatched to represent people. By tracing cut out figures from magazines and using this drawing technique students can make similar images.

Art Concept: Line. Repetition to create unity

Materials. Paper
Pencils
Black pens or markers
Scissors
Magazines

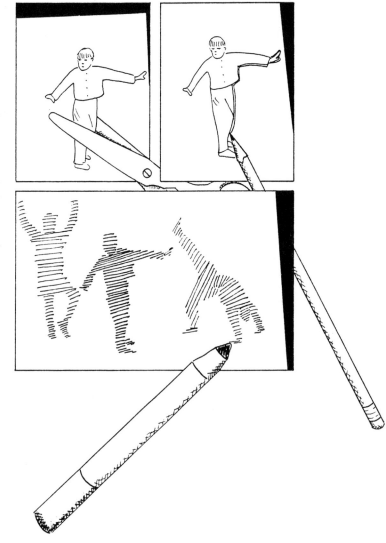

Instructions.

1. Have students look through magazines and find pictures of people. Cut the figures out.

2. Lay the cut shape on top of the drawing paper and lightly trace around it with pencil.

3. Fill in the shape with lines using a marker or a black pen.

From *Art Through Children's Literature*. ©1994. Teacher Ideas Press, P.O. Box 6633, Englewood, CO 80155-6633, 1-800-237-6124.

Cinderella, or the Little Glass Slipper
Illustrated and translated by Marcia Brown
Written by Charles Perrault
(New York: Scribner, 1954)
1955 Caldecott Award Winner

A romantic tale about a young girl, her stepfamily, and a prince.

Cinderella Drawing
Using light, wispy lines similar to the type the artist used students can draw their own version of Cinderella.

Art Concept: Line. Used to make a drawing with an expressive quality

Materials.   Paper
Pencils
Black markers
Crayons

Instructions.
1. Have the students begin their drawing with pencil. Then draw light and wispy lines with a marker, and add color with crayons.

From *Art Through Children's Literature*. ©1994. Teacher Ideas Press, P.O. Box 6633, Englewood, CO 80155-6633, 1-800-237-6124.

Cinderella, or the Little Glass Slipper
Illustrated and translated by Marcia Brown
Written by Charles Perrault
(New York: Scribner, 1954)
1955 Caldecott Award Winner

A romantic tale about a young girl, her stepfamily, and a prince.

Stepsister Drawing

The lines in the story's drawings have an expressive quality. Notice the type of line used in Cinderella's dress compared to her stepsisters'. Cinderella's dress is drawn with free-flowing lines that are light and wispy, but the stepsisters' dresses have heavier, almost scribbled-looking lines. Have the students use this method to draw their own version of one of the stepsisters.

Art Concept: Line. Used to make a drawing with an expressive quality

Materials. Paper
Pencils
Black markers
Crayons

Instructions.

1. Have students begin drawing the basic shape of one of the stepsisters with a pencil. Scribbled lines can be drawn with a marker for the dress and hair, and color can be added with crayons.

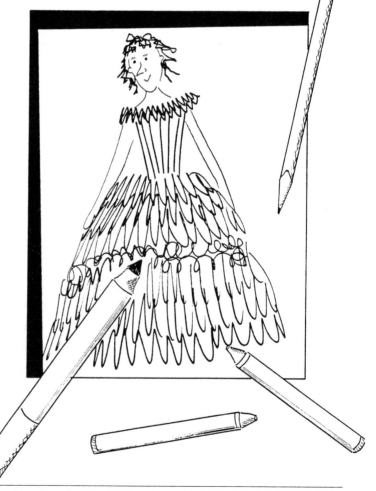

Duffy and the Devil
Illustrated by Margot Zemach
Retold by Harve Zemach
(New York: Farrar, 1973)
1974 Caldecott Award Winner

A variation of the story Rumpelstiltskin with an unusual ending.

Devil with a Shadow

Notice the illustration of the devil when he first appears to Duffy; his body casts a shadow. Students can make a drawing of a devil with a shadow by tracing around a drawing with a black marker and then applying water to the marker so that it bleeds and forms a shadow.

Art Concept: Shadow. Dark area around an object

Materials.   Paper
Water-based markers
Pencils
Water
Brushes

Instructions.
1. Have the students use a pencil to draw the shape of a devil.

2. Using markers, color the devil. Use a black marker to outline one side of the shape, then paint the black outline with water so that it spreads, forming a shadow.

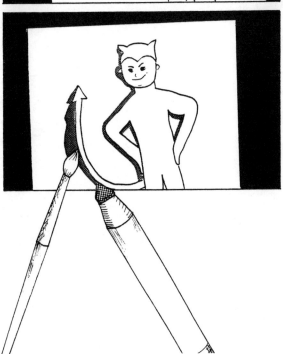

Finders Keepers
Illustrated by Nicolas [Nicolas Mordvinoff]
Written by Will [William Lipkind]
(New York: Harcourt, Brace, 1951)
1952 Caldecott Award Winner

Two dogs find a bone and learn a lesson about sharing.

Line Drawing

Throughout the book the artist uses a variety of lines in the illustrations. By imitating this technique of using different types of lines, students can make a landscape drawing with marker.

Art Concept: Types of Line. Straight, curved, organic, geometric, contour, and interior

Materials. Paper
Markers

Instructions.

1. Review the types of lines with students, then find examples of them in the story's illustrations. Have students draw, with markers, a landscape and instruct them to work with the various types of lines.

The Fool of the World and the Flying Ship
Illustrated by Uri Shulevitz
Retold by Arthur Ransome
(New York: Farrar, 1968)
1969 Caldecott Award Winner

When the Czar proclaims that he will marry his daughter to the man who brings
him a flying ship, the Fool of the World sets out to try his luck and meets
some unusual companions along the way.

Decorative Column

Examine the illustration of the fool's meeting with the Czar and the princess. Notice the patterned designs that decorate the columns. Using markers the students can design their own column.

Art Concepts:

Pattern. Repetition of shape.

Column. Made up of three main parts—the base, capital, and shaft

Materials. Paper
Pencils
Markers

Instructions.

1. Discuss with the class the decorative columns used to hold the large arches in the palace. Ask them to draw a column with a pencil.

2. Add patterns to the column using markers.

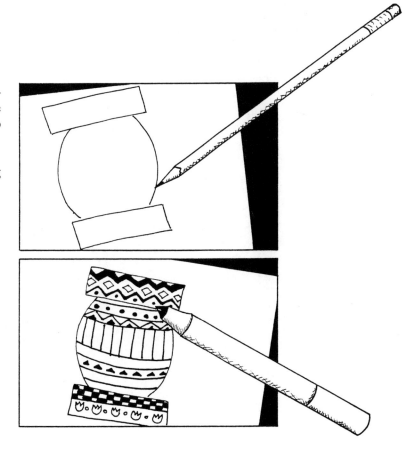

Frog Went A-Courtin'
Illustrated by Feodor Rojankovsky
Retold by John Langstaff
(New York: Harcourt, Brace, 1955)
1956 Caldecott Award Winner

A story based upon a song about the wedding of a frog and a mouse.

Bumblebee Drawing

Look carefully at the illustration of the bumblebee, noting the textures of the different parts of the body. Using a fine-point marker, students can draw their own version of a bumblebee.

Art Concept: Texture. Surface quality of an object

Materials. Paper
Pencils
Fine-point markers
Crayons

Instructions.

1. Have students begin by drawing the basic shape of the bee with a pencil.

2. Continue working with the pencil to add more details.

3. Use a black marker to draw over the top of the pencil lines, then add areas of texture using the marker and a crayon.

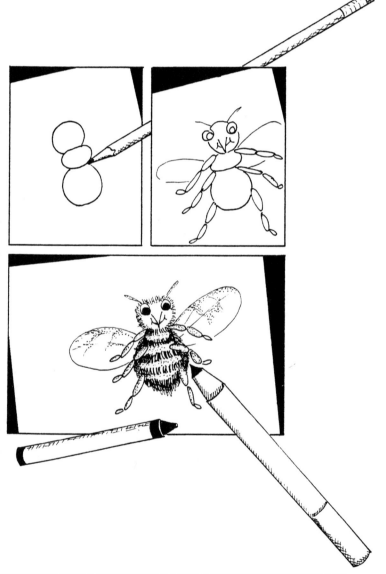

Frog Went A-Courtin'
Illustrated by Feodor Rojankovsky
Retold by John Langstaff
(New York: Harcourt, Brace, 1955)
1956 Caldecott Award Winner

A story based upon a song about the wedding of a frog and a mouse.

Cat Drawing

In the story, the last guest to arrive at the wedding is the cat. Examine the strokes the artist used to draw the cat. The students may make an illustration of the cat peeking through the leaves with similar line quality by combining crayon and marker.

Art Concept: Strokes. Used as an expressive element

Materials. Paper
Pencils
Black crayons
Markers

Instructions.
1. Have students begin by drawing two cat eyes with a pencil. Next draw a nose and a mouth, then place two ear shapes above the eyes.

2. Using a black crayon, outline the shapes drawn with pencil. Next add whiskers and fur using small strokes.

3. Continue adding fur with the markers. Leaves can be added to the background if desired.

From *Art Through Children's Literature*. ©1994. Teacher Ideas Press, P.O. Box 6633, Englewood, CO 80155-6633, 1-800-237-6124.

Owl Moon
Illustrated by John Schoenherr
Written by Jane Yolen
(New York: Philomel, 1987)
1988 Caldecott Award Winner

On a cold winter's night under a full moon, a father and daughter trek
into the woods to see the Great Horned Owl.

Owl Drawing

To show the texture of the owl the artist uses a variety of repeated lines. Students can draw an owl
with a black pen or marker and use lines to create texture.

Art Concept: Texture. Using repetition of line to give the appearance of feathers

Materials. Paper
Pencils
Black pens or black
    markers

Instructions.

1. Have students begin with an oval
    shape drawn with a pencil.

2. Draw to large circles inside of the
    oval for the eye area.

3. Draw the wings.

4. Sketch the beak, claws, eyes, and a
    branch for the owl to sit on.

5. Using a pen or marker, begin draw-
    ing lines around the eyes, then draw
    other areas of the owl using re-
    peated lines.

They Were Strong and Good
By Robert Lawson
(New York: Viking, 1940)
1941 Caldecott Award Winner

A story about the author's ancestors and how they helped build America.

Factory Drawing

To show depth in the drawing of the city of Paterson the artist draws the buildings in the foreground with more details; those in the background have fewer details and appear as groups of lines drawn in the shapes of buildings. Using lines drawn with a pen or marker, students may draw a group of factories.

Art Concept: Space. Achieved by drawing objects in the background with less clarity

Materials. Paper
Pencils
Pens or markers

Instructions.

1. Have the students lightly draw, with pencil, the shape of factories, placing larger shapes at the bottom of the picture. Small shapes should be placed at the top. Outline the shapes with a marker or pen. Add details such as windows, but remember that the nearer larger buildings should have more details than the ones in the distance.

Where the Wild Things Are
By Maurice Sendak
(New York: Harper & Row, 1963)
1964 Caldecott Award Winner

Max is sent to bed without his supper and dreams he is the king of the wild things.

Bedroom Forest

By varying the proximity of the lines, the artist shows areas of value in the illustrations. Using this technique students may make a drawing of their bedrooms turning into a forest as Max's room did.

Art Concept: Linear Value. Lines grouped together to achieve areas of light and dark

Materials.   Paper
Pencils
Fine-point markers

Instructions.

1. Have students begin by using a pencil to draw the side view of a bed.

2. Next, have students add trees to the bed.

3. Use a marker to add areas of value with small lines, spacing the lines close together for dark areas and farther apart for lighter areas.

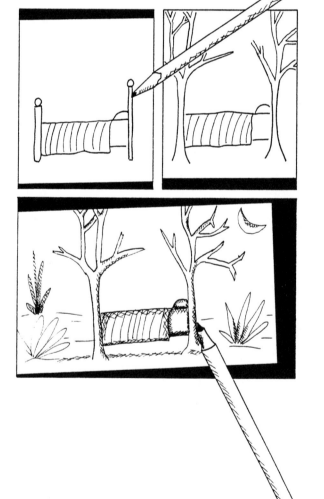

From *Art Through Children's Literature*. ©1994. Teacher Ideas Press, P.O. Box 6633, Englewood, CO 80155-6633, 1-800-237-6124.

Where the Wild Things Are
By Maurice Sendak
(New York: Harper & Row, 1963)
1964 Caldecott Award Winner

Max is sent to bed without his supper and dreams he is the king of the wild things.

Fantasy Animals

Look at the wild things from Max's imagination. Students may take parts of several animals and combine them into a wild thing from their imagination. Hatching and crosshatching can be used to give the flat shapes three-dimensional form.

Art Concepts:

Hatching. Shading with fine lines placed close together

Crosshatching. Placing lines that crisscross atop lines that are hatched

Materials.
Paper
Fine-point markers or
    pens
Pencils

Instructions.
1. Have students take parts from several different animals and combine them into one creature. Draw the shapes with pencil and add, with a fine-point marker, shaded areas drawn with hatched and crosshatched lines.

Chapter
4

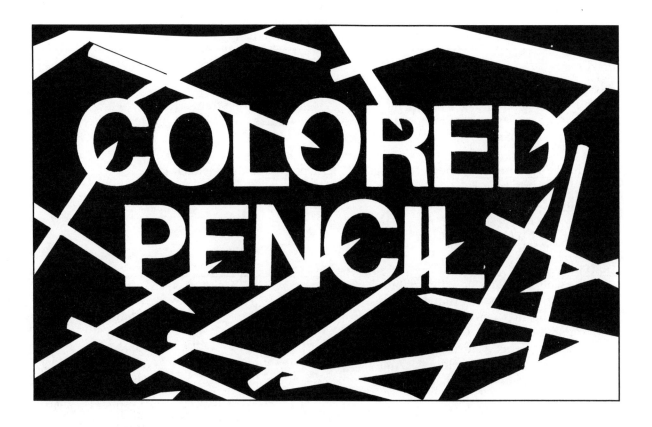

COLORED PENCIL

Colored pencil combines the qualities of pencil and crayon into one tool. The lessons in this chapter explore colored pencil using a variety of stroke applications to achieve different looks. They include drawing with lines, coloring in areas, and cross-hatching.

Abraham Lincoln
By Ingri and Edgar Parin d'Aulaire
(New York: Doubleday, 1939)
1940 Caldecott Award Winner

The story of a great president from his boyhood on the edge of the
wilderness to the Civil War and the Emancipation Proclamation.

Map Design

Look at the illustration of the map in the story. Notice how the artist frames the flat, two-dimensional
drawing with trees that have been shaded to look three-dimensional. Using this technique, students
may make a map design.

Art Concept: Shading. Dark areas that give a shape a three-dimensional look

Materials.　Paper
　　　　　　　Pencils
　　　　　　　Colored pencils

Instructions.
1.　Provide the students with a photo-
　　copy of a map. Instruct them to
　　trace the map on their paper and
　　frame the drawing with shaded ob-
　　jects. Students may draw objects
　　such as cars and buildings. Add
　　color with a colored pencil.

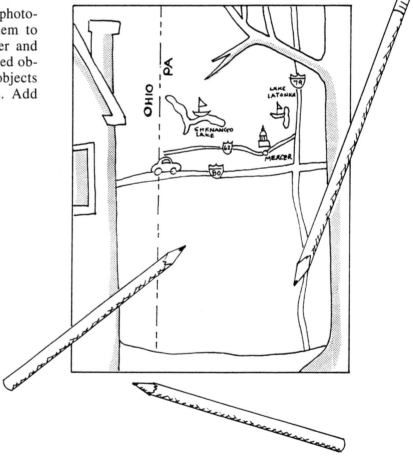

Abraham Lincoln
By Ingri and Edgar Parin d'Aulaire
(New York: Doubleday, 1939)
1940 Caldecott Award Winner

The story of a great president from his boyhood on the edge of the
wilderness to the Civil War and the Emancipation Proclamation.

Sunset Drawing
Look closely at the illustration of the sunset, noting the streaks of red and yellow that are
drawn next to each other. Close up the two colors are more apparent, but from a distance the
colors blend to make orange. Students can use colored pencils to draw a sunset.

Art Concepts:

Secondary Colors. Made from
mixing equal amounts of primary
colors. Red plus yellow equals
orange. Blue plus yellow equals
green. Blue plus red equals purple.

Optical Mix. Colors placed side
by side are mixed visually

Materials. Colored pencils:
red, yellow, and blue
White paper

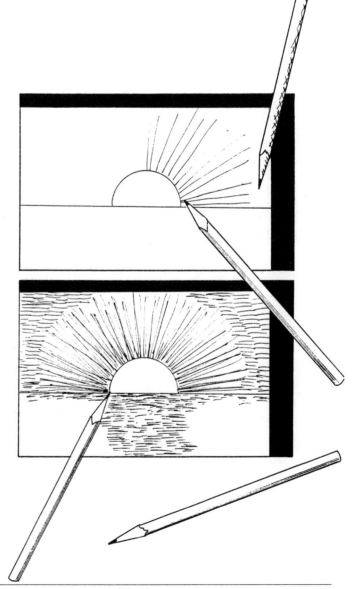

Instructions.
1. Have the students begin by drawing a blue line across the paper.
   Draw half of a circle above the line.
   Using a yellow pencil, have students draw lines radiating from the
   half circle.

2. Place red lines next to and on top
   of the yellow lines, and add color
   to the half circle using red and yellow colored pencils. Color the
   grass by combining yellow and
   blue.

From *Art Through Children's Literature*. ©1994. Teacher Ideas Press, P.O. Box 6633, Englewood, CO 80155-6633, 1-800-237-6124.

Saint George and the Dragon
Illustrated by Trina Schart Hyman
Retold by Margaret Hodges
(Boston: Little, Brown, 1984)
1985 Caldecott Award Winner

Retells a segment from Spenser's *The Faerie Queen*, in which George, the Red Cross Knight,
slays the dreadful dragon that has been terrorizing the countryside for years,
thereby bringing peace and joy to the land.

Dragon Letters

Notice the letters in the book's title. The artist has stylized the alphabet to fit the theme of the book.
Using this method, students may write their own names using a dragon motif.

Art Concept: Stylized. Artists change the usual look of an object to fit their own idea of how it
should look

Materials.   Paper
Pencils
Colored Pencils

Instructions.

1. Have students draw their names
lightly with pencil.

2. Add dragon parts to the letters, and
color these new shapes with colored
pencils.

Saint George and the Dragon
Illustrated by Trina Schart Hyman
Retold by Margaret Hodges
(Boston: Little, Brown, 1984)
1985 Caldecott Award Winner

Retells a segment from Spenser's *The Faerie Queen*, in which George, the Red Cross Knight,
slays the dreadful dragon that has been terrorizing the countryside for years,
thereby bringing peace and joy to the land.

View from a Window
Students may draw their own version of a dragon using pencil and colored pencil. Strips of construction paper may be used to frame the drawing and give the appearance of looking through a window—a technique that gives the illusion of depth.

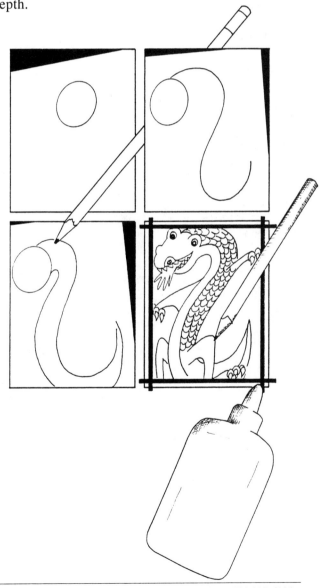

Art Concept: Depth. Created by placing a dominant object over other shapes

Materials. 12-x-18-inch paper
Pencils
Colored pencils
½-x-12-inch construction paper, two per student
½-x-18-inch construction paper, two per student
Glue

Instructions.
1. Discuss with the students what animals the image of a dragon could be conceived from: dinosaurs, snakes, lizards, or alligators. Demonstrate drawing a dragon for the class. Using pencil, draw an oval for the head.

2. Next draw a backward *S* line.

3. Repeat the backward *S* line, but space this second one away from the first.

4. Using colored pencils, add such details as arms, legs, wings, eyes, teeth, and scales, and glue the strips of ½-x-12-inch and ½-x-18-inch strips of paper over the finished drawing to frame it.

Song and Dance Man
Illustrated by Stephen Gammell
Written by Karen Ackerman
(New York: Knopf, 1988)
1989 Caldecott Award Winner

Grandpa's attic is transformed into a vaudeville stage where he performs for his grandchildren.

Colored-Pencil Silhouette
Using a cutout figure from a magazine, students can trace the outline of the shape to make a silhouette. Colored pencil may be used to make interior lines to achieve a look similar to the silhouette of the song-and-dance man beginning the old soft shoe.

Art Concept: Interior Lines. Series of crosshatched lines used to fill in a shape

Materials.   Paper
Pencils
Colored pencils
Scissors
Old magazines

Instructions.

1. Have students select a picture of a person from a magazine and cut the figure out. Place the figure on a sheet of drawing paper, and trace the outline with a pencil. Using colored pencil, color the inside of the figure with a series of cross-hatched lines.

Song and Dance Man
Illustrated by Stephen Gammell
Written by Karen Ackerman
(New York: Knopf, 1988)
1989 Caldecott Award Winner

Grandpa's attic is transformed into a vaudeville stage where he performs for his grandchildren.

Everyday Object
Throughout the book the artist used obvious pencil strokes in the illustrations. Many colors are overlapped to create the colorful drawings. Using this method students may draw a simple object such as a chair or lamp and achieve a look similar to the artist's.

Art Concept: Pencil Strokes. Used as an expressive element

Materials. Paper
Pencils
Colored pencils

Instructions.
1. Have students draw, with a pencil, the shape of an everyday object. Students may add lines of color to the drawing with a colored pencil.

Song and Dance Man
Illustrated by Stephen Gammell
Written by Karen Ackerman
(New York: Knopf, 1988)
1989 Caldecott Award Winner

Grandpa's attic is transformed into a vaudeville stage where he performs for his grandchildren.

Staircase Drawing

Look at the manner in which the artist grouped lines together to draw areas of light and dark in the story's illustrations. Working with a similar drawing technique, students may make their own staircase using colored pencil.

__Art Concept: Linear Value__. Grouping lines together to achieve areas of light and dark

__Materials__.   Paper
Pencils
Colored pencils

Instructions.

1. Have students begin their illustrations of a staircase by drawing the side and the top of a door frame very lightly with pencil.

2. Then draw the door and steps.

3. Using colored pencils, outline the shapes and begin adding areas of color. To draw the lighter areas of the picture, use a single color. Darker areas may be made by overlapping the lines from several colors.

Chapter

5

$\mathbf{L}$essons in this chapter combine chalk with other materials such as stencils, crayon, torn paper, and pencil. Chalk is a soft material that may be used to achieve a variety of looks. Thin lines may be made by using the end of the tool; for wide lines or broad areas, use the side of the chalk. Colors may be easily blended.

The Glorious Flight:
Across the Channel with Louis Blériot
By Alice and Martin Provensen
(New York: Viking, 1983)
1984 Caldecott Award Winner

A biography of the man whose fascination with flying machines produced the Blériot XI, which crossed the English Channel in thirty-seven minutes in the early 1900s.

Lost in the Fog

To illustrate the airplane lost in the fog, the artist shows a very small plane compared to the size of the surrounding sky. Students may draw Blériot's plane lost in the fog by using size as a key element.

Art Concept: Size. Used as an expressive element

Materials.   Dark construction paper
Pencils
Crayons
Chalk

Instructions.

1. Have students draw, with pencil, a very small airplane on their paper.

2. Color the plane with crayons.

3. Using the side of a piece of chalk, add areas of fog.

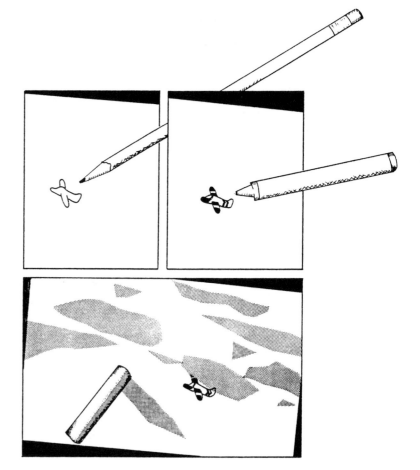

Lon Po Po:
A Red-Riding Hood Story from China
By Ed Young
(New York: Philomel, 1989)
1990 Caldecott Award Winner

Three sisters staying home alone are endangered by a hungry
wolf who is disguised as their grandmother.

Blended-Chalk Design
Throughout the book the artist combines detailed drawings with drawings that simply suggest various objects. Have the class look at the drawing where the three girls climb the ginkgo tree. The girls are drawn with more detail than the tree's leaves, the shapes of which are only suggested. Using chalk, the students may create a similar image of a tree.

<u>Art Concept: Abstracted</u>. A recognizable shape that has been simplified

<u>Materials</u>.   Colored construction
         paper
       Pencils
       Crayons
       Chalk

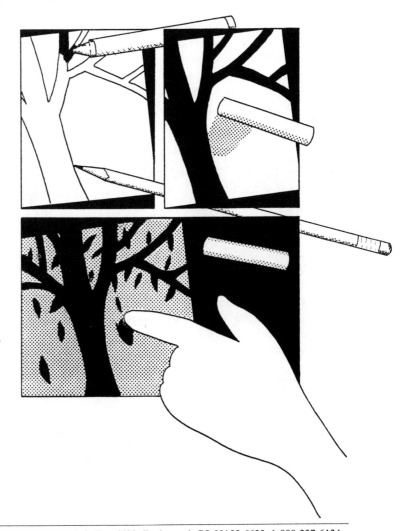

<u>Instructions</u>.
1. Discuss the possible shape of the leaves before they were simplified. Begin the picture by drawing the trunk and branches of a tree with pencil on colored construction paper. Color the trunk and branches with a dark crayon.

2. Lay a green piece of chalk on its side and color the entire background.

3. Select additional chalk colors and apply small leaf shapes. Have the students rub gently over the leaf shapes with their fingers to blend the colors with the background.

Lon Po Po:
A Red-Riding Hood Story from China
By Ed Young
(New York: Philomel, 1989)
1990 Caldecott Award Winner

Three sisters staying home alone are endangered by a hungry
wolf who is disguised as their grandmother.

Chalk Landscape Drawing

The landscape at the beginning of the story has a soft quality. By using the rubbing technique described below, students may create a landscape design with qualities similar to what the artist achieved.

Art Concept: Chalk. A soft material that blends easily to create soft images

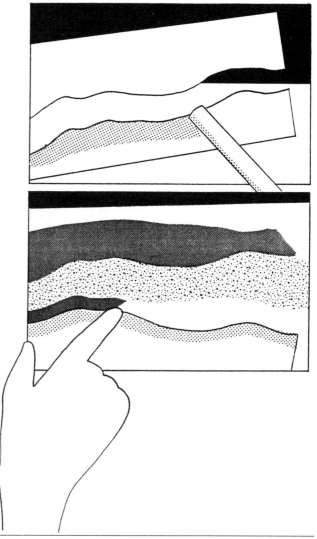

Materials. 4½-x-12-inch con-
       struction paper
9-x-12-inch colored
       construction paper
Chalk in assorted colors
       if available
Newspaper

Instructions.

1. Have each student tear a 4½-x-12-inch piece of construction paper into two long strips. Lay the strips on a sheet of newspaper and color heavily with chalk on the torn edge.

2. Lay the coated strip on top of a sheet of 9-x-12-inch construction paper, and rub the chalk from the torn paper to the construction paper. Add more chalk to the torn paper and repeat the rubbing in new locations.

Lon Po Po:
A Red-Riding Hood Story from China
By Ed Young
(New York: Philomel, 1989)
1990 Caldecott Award Winner

Three sisters staying home alone are endangered by a hungry
wolf who is disguised as their grandmother.

Crayon-and-Chalk Shadow Drawing

In the story, the candle blows out as the wolf enters the house. Notice the shadow cast by the wolf.
By combining chalk and crayon students may make a shadow drawing.

Art Concept: Chalk-and-Crayon Drawing. Combining two types of materials in one picture

Materials.   Colored construction
               paper
         Pencils
         Chalk in assorted colors
         Black crayons

Instructions.
1. Have the students select a color of background paper, but remind them that some of that color will show through the chalk. Then with a pencil draw the outline of a person or animal. Using the black crayon, color in the shape. With the side of a piece of chalk, color over the entire paper including the crayon drawing. Instruct students to rub the chalk with their fingers to blend evenly.

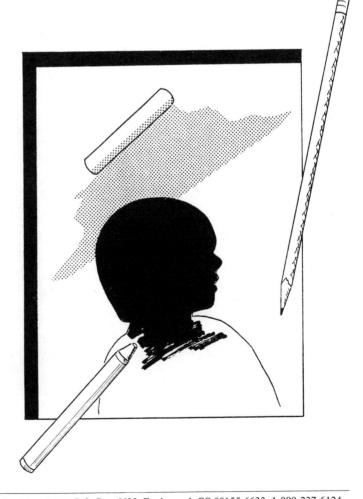

Nine Days to Christmas
Illustrated by Marie Hall Ets
Written by Marie Hall Ets and Aurora Labastida
(New York: Viking, 1959)
1960 Caldecott Award Winner

A Mexican girl named Ceci chooses a special pinata for the Christmas celebration.

Buildings at Night

To suggest nighttime in the story the artist uses a bright color on the windows. Using chalk and pencil on gray paper students may draw a building at night that has windows with a brighter intensity than the rest of the picture.

Art Concept: Intensity. Brightness or dullness

Materials. Gray paper
Pencils
White or yellow chalk

Instructions.
1. Instruct students to draw a building or buildings on a sheet of gray paper with pencil. Using chalk, they should then color the windows to give them a brighter intensity.

From *Art Through Children's Literature*. ©1994. Teacher Ideas Press, P.O. Box 6633, Englewood, CO 80155-6633, 1-800-237-6124.

The Polar Express
By Chris Van Allsburg
(Boston: Houghton Mifflin, 1985)
1986 Caldecott Award Winner

A magical train ride on Christmas Eve takes a boy to the North Pole to
receive a special gift from Santa Claus.

Christmas Ornament

To give the shapes in the illustrations a three-dimensional form, the artist uses highlights and shades.
Students may make a Christmas ornament with form by using chalk and a stencil.

Art Concepts:

Highlight. Area of brightest value

Shade. Area of dark value

Materials.   Oak tag
Dark-colored construction paper
White or yellow chalk
Scissors
Scrap paper

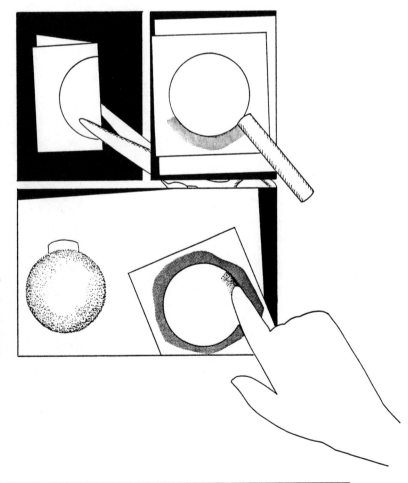

Instructions.

1. Have students fold a piece of oak tag or heavy paper in half. With chalk draw a half circle on the fold, and cut the circle out to make a stencil.

2. Place the stencil on top of a piece of scrap paper. Pressing heavily with chalk the students should trace around the edge of the stencil.

3. Place the coated stencil on top of the construction paper. Using their fingers have students rub the chalk from the edge of the stencil to the paper. Remove the stencil, and draw the top of the ornament.

From *Art Through Children's Literature*. ©1994. Teacher Ideas Press, P.O. Box 6633, Englewood, CO 80155-6633, 1-800-237-6124.

The Polar Express
By Chris Van Allsburg
(Boston: Houghton Mifflin, 1985)
1986 Caldecott Award Winner

A magical train ride on Christmas Eve takes a boy to the North Pole to
receive a special gift from Santa Claus.

Polar Express on the Mountain

Examine the illustration in the story of the Polar Express as it travels up the mountain. The side of
the mountain lighted by the moon has a brighter intensity than the side in the shadow. Using crayon
on colored construction paper, students may draw the Polar Express on the mountain.

Art Concept: Intensity. Brightness or dullness of a color

Materials. Black construction paper
Pencils
Crayons
White chalk

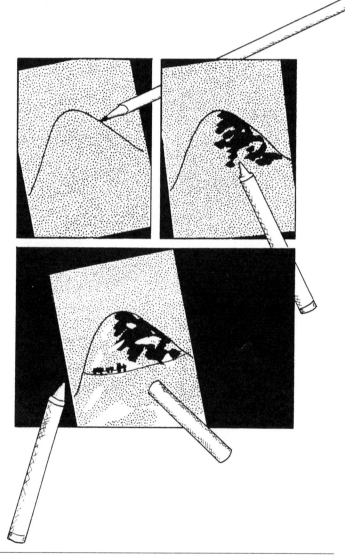

Instructions.

1. Have the students draw with a pencil the shape of a mountain on the
   construction paper.

2. Suggest a dark color of crayon to
   color one side of the mountain.

3. Color the entire mountain with
   white chalk. The white will be
   more intense on the side that does
   not have the dark color underneath.
   Complete the drawing by adding
   the Polar Express climbing the
   mountain.

From *Art Through Children's Literature*. ©1994. Teacher Ideas Press, P.O. Box 6633, Englewood, CO 80155-6633, 1-800-237-6124.

Sylvester and the Magic Pebble
By William Steig
(New York: Simon & Schuster, 1969)
1970 Caldecott Award Winner

In a moment of fright, Sylvester the donkey asks his magic pebble to turn him into a rock, but then cannot hold the pebble to wish himself back to normal again.

Sylvester in the Cool Night

To illustrate nighttime, the artist uses cool colors. Students may use chalk to make their own drawing of Sylvester and the pebble in the night.

Art Concept: Cool Colors. Colors in which blue is dominant—the violet-green half of the color wheel

Materials.   Blue construction paper
Pencils
Chalk

Instructions.
1. Review the cool and warm colors with students. Using blue construction paper and a pencil, draw Sylvester and the pebble. Add trees, hills, and stars.

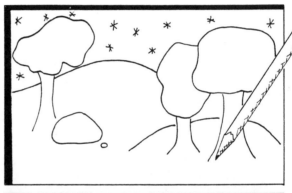

2. Using the cool colors, add color to the picture with chalk. Notice that the illustration in the book shows colors blended together. Imitate this look by rubbing the chalk.

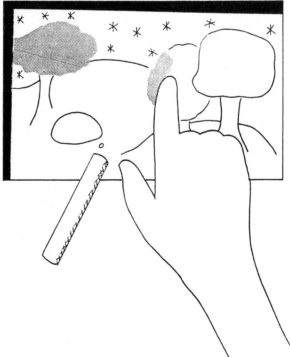

Chapter
6

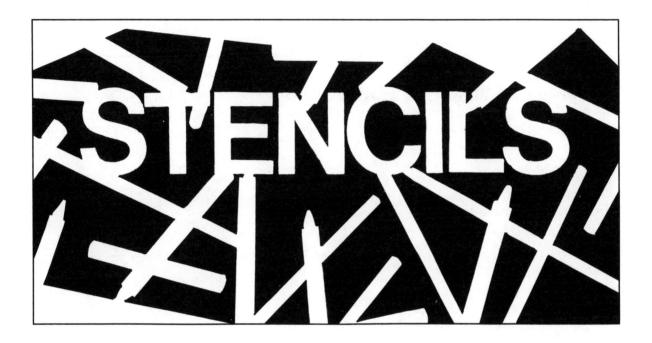

T raditional stenciling is a method of creating a number of images from one shape that has been cut into wax-coated paper. Paint is dabbed through the opening and the image appears on the background surface. The stencil technique explored in this chapter is a similar process, but uses heavyweight paper or oak tag in place of the wax-coated paper. Pencil, crayon, and chalk are used in place of paint to make the images.

Ashanti to Zulu: African Traditions
Illustrated by Leo and Diane Dillon
Written by Margaret Musgrove
(New York: Dial, 1976)
1977 Caldecott Award Winner

Traditions and customs of various African peoples are explored
in paragraphs which begin with letters from A to Z.

Positive and Negative Map Design

The map in the book has a patterned background that is the negative space. The positive shape of land appears almost as a hole in the patterned design. Using a photocopy of a map, students may make their own patterned map design.

Art Concept: Negative Shapes. The space created around the actual object

Materials.   Photocopies of maps
Paper
Pencils
Scissors

Instructions.

1. Photocopy a variety of maps, and let the students select the one they would like to use. Cut out the land shapes. Place the shapes on paper, and trace them with pencil.

2. Around these outlines of land shapes use a pencil to draw the patterned background, which creates the positive and negative spaces.

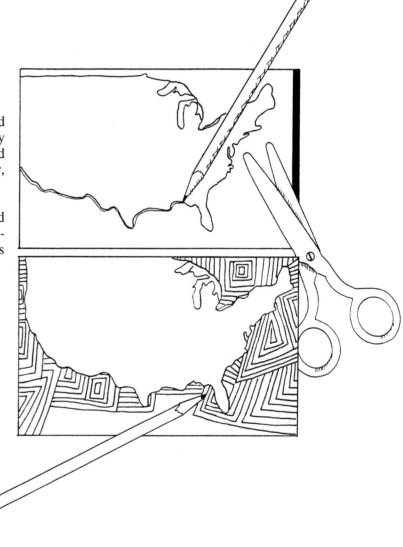

From *Art Through Children's Literature*. ©1994. Teacher Ideas Press, P.O. Box 6633, Englewood, CO 80155-6633, 1-800-237-6124.

The Big Snow
By Berta and Elmer Hader
(New York: Macmillan, 1948)
1949 Caldecott Award Winner

A story about animals preparing for the winter snow.

Rainbow Around the Moon

Using pencil and a circle cut out of paper students may make a drawing of the moon as it appears when the owl warns of more snow to come.

Art Concept: Stencil. Used to block out an area on paper

Materials. Paper
Pencils
Paper circles

Instructions.

1. Provide each student with a paper circle, and ask them to place the shape on the white paper. Have students use a pencil to make small strokes side by side around the entire circle.

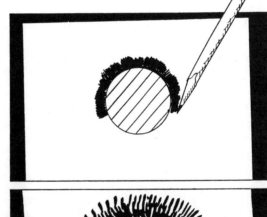

2. Make another row of small strokes around the first row, continuing with row after row until the paper is filled. Students may rub their finger over the rings to make the pencil strokes softer.

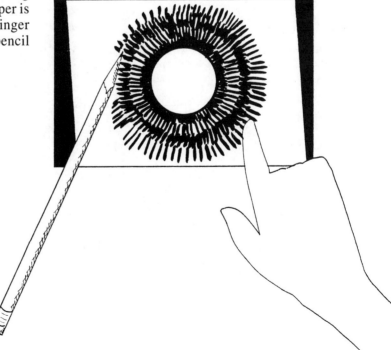

From *Art Through Children's Literature*. ©1994. Teacher Ideas Press, P.O. Box 6633, Englewood, CO 80155-6633, 1-800-237-6124.

The Big Snow
By Berta and Elmer Hader
(New York: Macmillan, 1948)
1949 Caldecott Award Winner

A story about animals preparing for the winter snow.

Snow-Covered Pines

Examine the illustrations in the book of the snow covering the pine trees. The snow lays on the branches like small clouds with the needles of the tree peeking out. To give form to the snow shape the artist uses shading. The edge of the shape is shaded light gray, and the center is left white. This gives the flat shapes three-dimensional form. Students may make an illustration of the snow-covered pines by using a stencil technique and pencil.

Art Concepts:

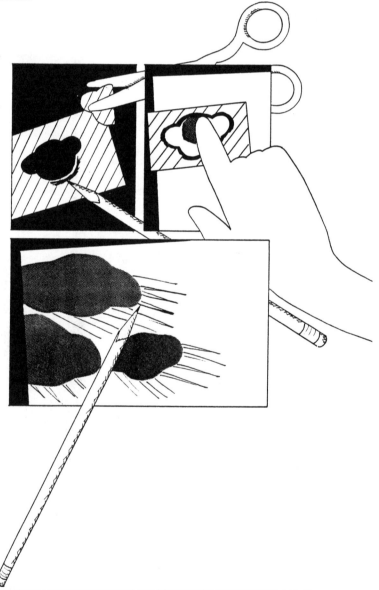

Form. An object's appearance of being three-dimensional

Shading. Adding dark areas to a shape to give it form

Materials.   Oak tag
Paper
Pencils
Scissors
Scrap paper

Instructions.

1. Provide each student with a sheet of oak tag or heavy paper, and ask them to fold the piece in half. Have them draw half of a cloud shape on the paper, and cut the shape out. Place the shape on a piece of scrap paper, then draw with pencil around the edge of the shape. Press hard to build up graphite.

2. Lay the cloud shape on top of the white paper. Instruct students to rub their fingers around the shape and onto the white paper without rubbing the center, which should remain white.

3. Draw pine needles under the cloud shape, and include additional shapes to form a tree.

From *Art Through Children's Literature.* ©1994. Teacher Ideas Press, P.O. Box 6633, Englewood, CO 80155-6633, 1-800-237-6124.

Black and White
By David Macaulay
(Boston: Houghton Mifflin, 1990)
1991 Caldecott Award Winner

Words and pictures tell four stories at one time about a train, cows, commuters, and parents.

Cows at Night

The shape of the cows begins to break up in the darkness, and only small parts of their forms remain recognizable. Stencils can be used with white crayon on black paper to achieve a similar look.

Art Concept: Abstracted. The simplification of a recognizable image

Materials. Photocopied picture of a cow
Black construction paper
White crayons
Oak tag
Scissors
Glue

Instructions.

1. Provide each student with a photo-copied image of a cow and ask them to glue the photocopy onto a piece of oak tag or heavy construction paper.

2. After the glue has dried, instruct students to cut out the mounted cow shape.

3. Lay the stencil shape on top of the black paper. With a white crayon have students trace the outline of the stencil—not fully but in parts so that the outline resembles a cow seen only partially in the darkness. Draw over the stencil with white crayon. Place the stencil in a new location and repeat.

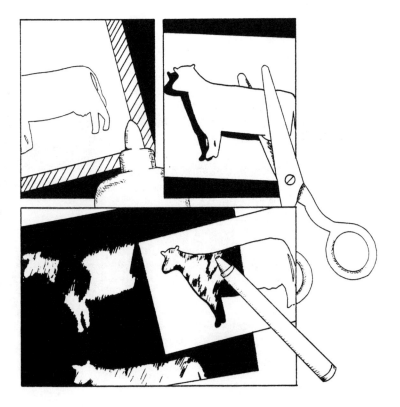

Jumanji
By Chris Van Allsburg
(Boston: Houghton Mifflin, 1981)
1982 Caldecott Award Winner

Left on their own for an afternoon, two bored and restless children find more
excitement than they bargained for in a mysterious and mystical
jungle adventure board game.

Three-Dimensional Drawing

Throughout the book the artist uses shading to give the shapes a three-dimensional quality. Using a
stencil, students may give form to a circle.

<u>Art Concept: Shading</u>. Coloring a shape in a manner to give it three-dimensional form

<u>Materials</u>.   4-x-4-inch oak tag or
            heavy paper
        Dark construction paper
        Newspaper or scrap paper
        Pencils
        Scissors
        Chalk

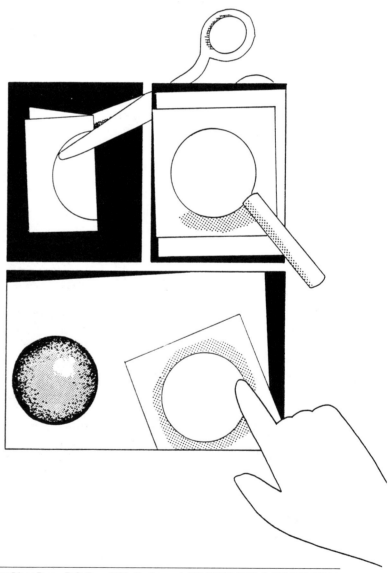

<u>Instructions</u>.
1. Provide each student with a piece
    of 4-x-4-inch oak tag or heavy pa-
    per. Instruct the students to fold the
    sheet in half. Draw and cut out a
    half circle on the fold.

2. Place the stencil shape on a piece of
    newspaper or scrap paper, and coat
    the edge with chalk.

3. Lay the coated shape on top of the
    dark construction paper, and in-
    struct the students to rub the chalk
    from the stencil to the paper.

Jumanji
By Chris Van Allsburg
(Boston: Houghton Mifflin, 1981)
1982 Caldecott Award Winner

Left on their own for an afternoon, two bored and restless children find more
excitement than they bargained for in a mysterious and mystical
jungle adventure board game.

Three-Dimensional Drawing with Details

Shading is often used to give flat objects a three-dimensional quality, and stencils may be used to
make these shaded objects. By combining two stencils the students may add details to a ball to give
it the appearance of a toy.

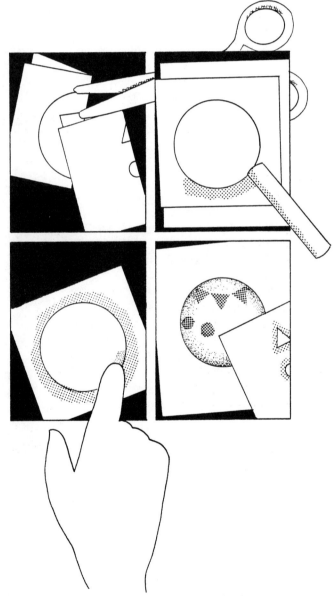

Art Concept: Shading. Coloring a
shape in a manner that gives it three-
dimensional form

Materials.   2 pieces of 4-x-4-inch oak
tag or heavy paper
Dark construction paper
Newspaper or scrap paper
Pencils
Scissors
Chalk

Instructions.

1. Provide each student with two
pieces of 4-x-4-inch oak tag or
heavy paper. Instruct them to fold
the sheets in half. On one piece of
the folded paper draw a half circle
on the fold; in the other, two
smaller shapes. Cut out the three
shapes.

2. Place the stencil shapes on a piece
of newspaper or scrap paper, and
coat the edges with chalk.

3. Lay the large, coated circle shape
on top of the dark construction
paper, and instruct the students to
rub the chalk from the stencil to the
paper.

4. Repeat the above step with the
smaller stencils.

Jumanji
By Chris Van Allsburg
(Boston: Houghton Mifflin, 1981)
1982 Caldecott Award Winner

Left on their own for an afternoon, two bored and restless children find more
excitement than they bargained for in a mysterious and mystical
jungle adventure board game.

Three-Dimensional House

Examine the illustration of the small playhouse in the story. Shading is used to give the house a three-dimensional look. By combining a number of stencils in one picture, students can make a house similar to the playhouse in the story.

Art Concept: Shading. Coloring a shape in a way that gives it three-dimensional form

Materials.   Oak tag or heavy paper
Drawing paper
Newspaper or scrap paper
Pencils
Scissors

Instructions.

1. Provide each student with several sheets of oak tag or heavy paper. Instruct them to draw and cut out the shapes needed for a house. Place the stencil shapes on a piece of newspaper or scrap paper, and coat the edges with pencil.

2. Lay the coated shapes on top of the white paper and rub them to transfer the images to form a house.

The Rooster Crows
By Maud and Miska Petersham
(New York: Macmillan, 1945)
1946 Caldecott Award Winner

A collection of rhymes and chants.

Cloud Rubbings

By using a method of blocking out areas on their drawings students may make cloud designs similar to those in the book.

<u>**Art Concept: Frisket**</u>. A shape cut from paper and placed on top of a drawing surface to block out part of the design so that the area remains blank

<u>**Materials**</u>. Paper
Pencils
Scraps of paper
Scissors

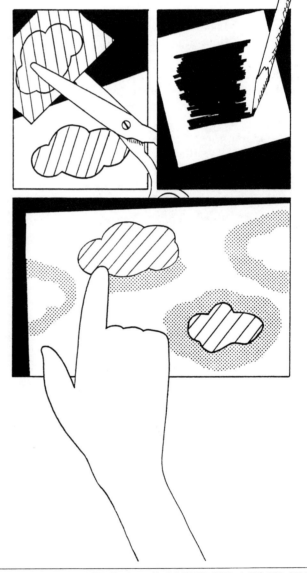

<u>**Instructions**</u>.

1. Ask the students to cut out cloud shapes using the scraps of paper, then place the clouds on the drawing paper.

2. Rub the pencil onto a piece of scrap paper in one area to build up excess graphite.

3. Have students coat their fingers with the excess graphite. Rub the material over the tops and around the sides of the cut out shapes. Remove the cloud shapes.

The Rooster Crows
By Maud and Miska Petersham
(New York: Macmillan, 1945)
1946 Caldecott Award Winner

A collection of rhymes and chants.

Mountain Design

Mountains similar to the ones in the rhyme "I have a little sister" can be drawn by shading with a pencil on the edge of a stencil.

<u>Art Concept: Shading</u>. Technique of drawing with a pencil and making areas of different value

<u>Materials</u>. Pencils
Paper
Oak tag
Scissors

<u>Instructions</u>.

1. Have each student cut a piece of oak tag or heavy paper into the shape of a mountain. Place the shape on top of a sheet of drawing paper. Using the side of a pencil, have them draw small strokes across the edge of the shape using a back-and-forth motion. Move the shape to a new spot and repeat.

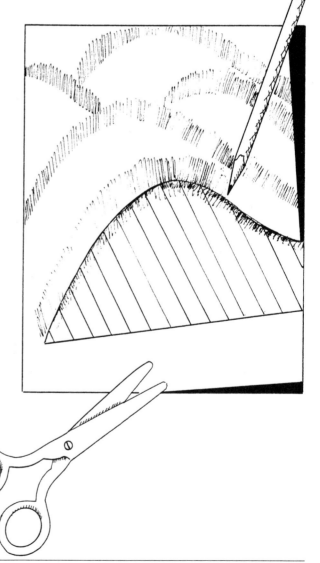

Shadow
Illustrated and translated by Marcia Brown
Written by Blaise Cendrars
(New York: Scribner, 1982)
1983 Caldecott Award Winner

Translated from the work by French poet Blaise Cendrars,
this story explores the mysterious world of shadows.

Smoke Design

Examine the illustration at the end of the story. Notice how the smoke overlaps to create depth. Through the use of stencils the students may overlap shapes to make a picture of flames and smoke.

<u>Art Concept: **Rhythm**</u>. Repeating colors and shapes to create a picture

<u>Materials</u>. Paper
Pencils
Crayons
Scissors
Oak tag

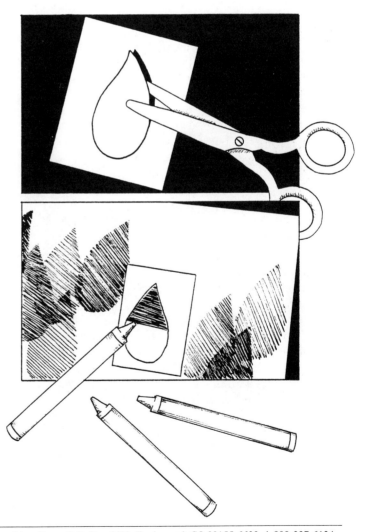

<u>Instructions</u>.
1. Provide each student with a piece of oak tag or heavy paper and have them draw a flame shape in the paper's center. Cut out the shape.

2. Lay the stencil over top of the drawing paper and color the flames, repeating the shape to make a design.

Why Mosquitoes Buzz in People's Ears
Illustrated by Leo and Diane Dillon
Retold by Verna Aardema
(New York: Dial, 1975)
1976 Caldecott Award Winner

A series of events occurs as a result of a mosquito's exaggerated story.

Animals with Patterned Markings

Look at the markings on the various animals in the story. Using a stencil and crayons, students may decorate the surface of an animal that they have cut out of colored construction paper.

Art Concept: Pattern. Repetition of shapes

Materials.   Colored construction
paper for the
background
Colored construction
paper for the animal
Oak tag for stencils
Scissors
Pencils
Crayons
Glue

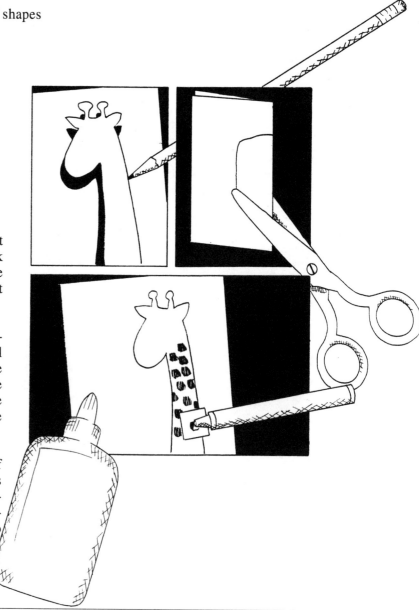

Instructions.

1.   Provide each student with a sheet of colored construction paper. Ask them to draw with a pencil the shape of an animal and then to cut it out.

2.   To decorate the animal with patterned markings the students will need to make a stencil using a piece of oak tag or heavy paper. Fold the oak tag in half, draw half of the shape on the fold, and cut the shape out.

3.   Glue the animal onto a piece of background paper. After it has dried, place the stencil over the animal shape and color within the stencil with crayon. Move the stencil to a new location and repeat.

Chapter
7

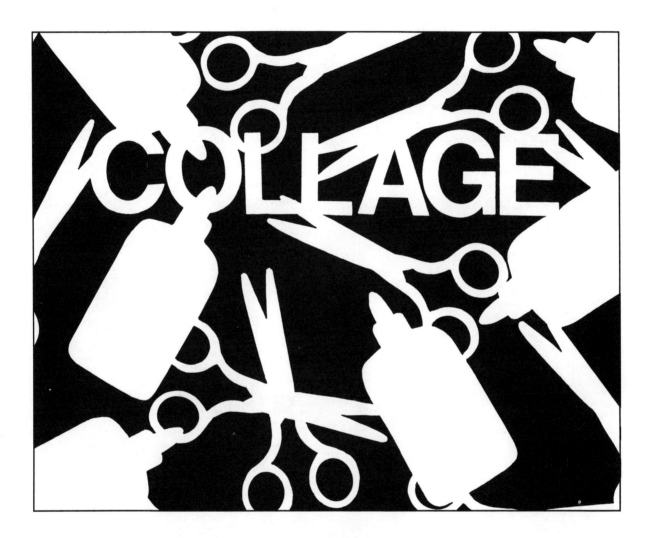

A collage is a two-dimensional design made by gluing materials to a background surface such as paper. This chapter explores collages made from construction paper, cotton, newspaper, old magazines, and tissue paper. The collages are also combined with crayons and markers.

Arrow to the Sun
By Gerald McDermott
(New York: Viking, 1974)
1975 Caldecott Award Winner

A Pueblo legend about an Indian boy's search for his father, the Sun.

Geometric Collage

Examine the illustrations of the Pueblo boy. Squares, rectangles, and triangles are used to make the figure. Students may make their own version of the Pueblo boy using geometric shapes.

Art Concept: Geometric Shapes. Circle, square, rectangle, and triangle

<u>Materials</u>. Colored construction
     paper for the
     background
    1- and 2-inch strips of
     colored construction
     paper
    Scissors
    Glue

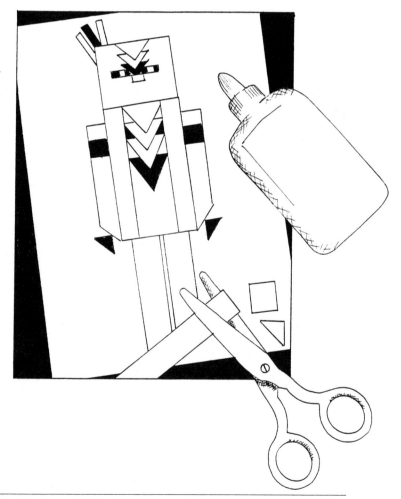

Instructions.

1. Let students select several strips of construction paper in different widths and colors, then ask them to cut the strips into squares, triangles, and rectangles. Arrange the shapes to make the Pueblo boy, and glue the shapes onto the background paper.

Arrow to the Sun
By Gerald McDermott
(New York: Viking, 1974)
1975 Caldecott Award Winner

A Pueblo legend about an Indian boy's search for his father, the Sun.

Mosaic Collage

Notice the type of stars the artist uses in the story. They represent how the artist imagined a star should look. Students may apply small pieces of paper to the surface of black paper to give the appearance of the stars in the sky.

Art Concept: Symbol. Shapes that represent what is in the artist's mind, not what actually exists in the world

Materials. Black construction paper for the background
¼-inch-wide strips of paper in assorted colors
Scrap paper for glue
Toothpicks
Scissors
Glue

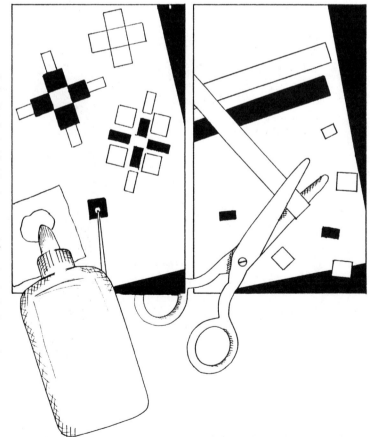

Instructions.
1. Show the students the illustration in the story where the arrow maker has shot the boy through the sky to the sun. Discuss with the students the shapes that are used to symbolize stars, then let each student select several ¼-inch strips of paper. Ask them to cut the strips into small squares and rectangles.

2. Instruct the students to place a small drop of glue on a piece of scrap paper. Dab the end of a toothpick into the glue, and place a small dot on the tiny cut out shape. Place the shape onto the black construction paper. Continue this process, making a variety of star shapes and sizes.

From *Art Through Children's Literature*. ©1994. Teacher Ideas Press, P.O. Box 6633, Englewood, CO 80155-6633, 1-800-237-6124.

Ashanti to Zulu: African Traditions
Illustrated by Leo and Diane Dillon
Written by Margaret Musgrove
(New York: Dial, 1976)
1977 Caldecott Award Winner

Traditions and customs of various African peoples are explored
in paragraphs which begin with letters from A to Z.

Landscape Collage
Notice the free-flowing shapes that the artist uses in the landscape illustration at the beginning of the story. Students can make a landscape collage using organic shapes.

Art Concept: Organic Shapes. Free-flowing forms

Materials.   Background paper
Scrap paper
Scissors
Glue

Instructions.
1. Ask the students to cut out organic shapes from scrap paper to create a landscape. Have them glue the pieces to the background paper.

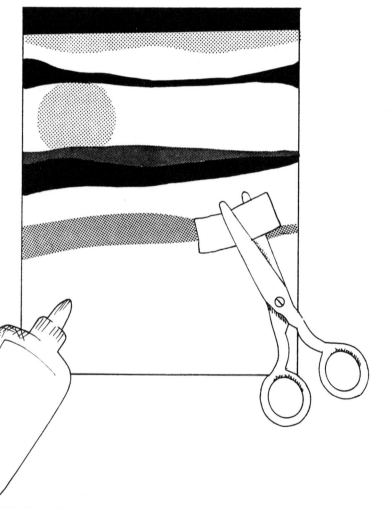

Baboushka and the Three Kings
Illustrated by Nicolas Sidjakov
Written by Ruth Robbins
(Berkeley, Calif.: Parnassus, 1960)
1961 Caldecott Award Winner

A Russian legend about a woman and her search for the Christ child.

Three Kings

Notice the illustrations of the people throughout the book. The shapes are simplified. Using geometric shapes, students can make similar figures.

<u>Art Concept: Shape</u>. Geometric shapes can be combined to form a figure

<u>Materials</u>. Colored construction paper for the background
Scraps of colored construction paper
Crayons
Scissors
Glue

<u>Instructions</u>.

1. Ask the students to use crayons to draw geometric shapes on scraps of construction paper to make up the parts of the king. Cut out the shapes, leaving the crayon line.

2. Have them glue the shapes onto the construction paper to form the figure. Repeat the above steps to make additional people.

Black and White
By David Macaulay
(Boston: Houghton Mifflin, 1990)
1991 Caldecott Award Winner

Words and pictures tell four stories at one time about a train, cows, commuters, and parents.

Word Collage

Examine the illustration in the story, "Seeing Things," in which the boy discovers strange creatures throwing paper into the air. Notice the words are placed to form the shape of two people. Words cut from a newspaper can be glued onto a background sheet in a similar manner to form the space around a person.

Art Concept: Positive and Negative Space. The actual shape of an object is the positive space, and the area around the actual shape is the negative space

Materials.   Colored construction
paper
Newspapers
Pencils
Scissors
Glue

Instructions.
1. Provide each student with several sections of newspaper and ask them to cut out words. In pencil lightly outline the shape of a figure on the colored construction paper.

2. Instruct the students to glue the cut-out words onto the paper around the drawn shape.

The Egg Tree
By Katherine Milhous
(New York: Scribner, 1950)
1951 Caldecott Award Winner

A family tradition of egg decorating is passed on.

Border Designs

Notice the borders in the story. Those that are symmetrical are the same on both sides of the center axis. But there are several borders that are not the same on both sides. They are asymmetrical. Students can create a symmetrical border with construction paper.

Art Concept: Symmetrical. A design that is the same on both sides of the center axis

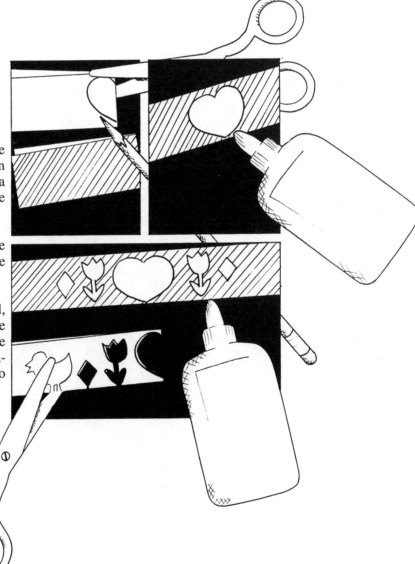

Materials. 6-x-18-inch colored
                   construction paper
             6-x-18-inch white paper
             Pencils
             Scissors
             Glue

Instructions.
1. Have the students fold the white paper and construction paper in half. Draw and cut out half of a shape in the center of the white paper.

2. Instruct the students to open the folded white shape and glue it to the center of the construction paper.

3. Keeping the white paper folded, students can draw and cut out more shapes. Glue the shapes onto the construction paper in the same location on both sides of the center to create a symmetrical design.

The Egg Tree
By Katherine Milhous
(New York: Scribner, 1950)
1951 Caldecott Award Winner

A family tradition of egg decorating is passed on.

Positive and Negative Egg

Notice the egg designs used in the border throughout the book. The egg is made of positive and negative shapes. Students may make an egg design that shows positive and negative shapes by cutting construction paper.

Art Concepts:

<u>Positive Shape</u>. Actual shape of an object

<u>Negative Shape</u>. Area around the positive shape

<u>Materials</u>.   12-x-18-inch colored
                      construction paper
              6-x-18-inch colored
                      construction paper
              Pencils
              Scissors
              Glue

Instructions.

1. Provide each student with a 12-x-18-inch and a 6-x-18-inch sheet of colored construction paper. Instruct the class to draw, with a pencil, half of an egg on the 6-x-18-inch paper. Draw a simple design on the egg, and carefully cut the shapes out.

2. Lay the egg shape on half of the 12-x-18-inch paper, and place all the cut pieces together like a puzzle. Flip every other piece over to the opposite side. Glue the pieces on both sides of the paper.

Fables
By Arnold Lobel
(New York: Harper & Row, 1980)
1981 Caldecott Award Winner

Twenty fables about an array of animal characters from
crocodile to ostrich, each containing a clever moral.

Flowers

In the story "The Crocodile in the Bedroom," Mr. Crocodile loved the order of the flowers on his wallpaper. The chaos of a real garden was overwhelming to him. Using construction paper students may make two flower designs: one ordered and one chaotic.

Art Concepts:

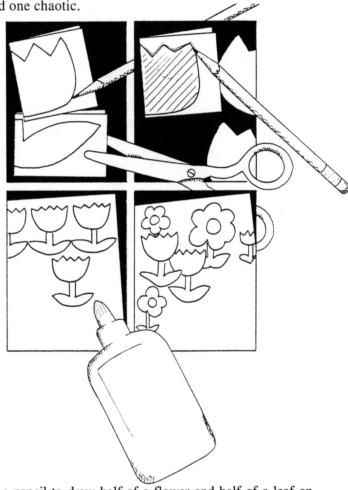

Pattern. Repetition of shape to show order

Chaos. Placement of objects in an unorganized manner

Materials. 9-x-12-inch colored
    construction paper
    for backgrounds
    (2 per student)
  2-x-3-inch colored
    construction paper
    for the petals
    (12 per student)
  1-x-3-inch green
    construction paper
    for the leaves
    (12 per student)
  Scraps of colored
    construction paper
  Glue
  Pencils
  Scissors

Instructions.

1. Provide each student with 12 sheets of 2-x-3-inch and 1-x-3-inch construction paper. Fold all the paper in half. Use a pencil to draw half of a flower and half of a leaf on the fold, then cut the flower and leaf shapes out.

2. Use the first shape as a pattern, and draw and cut out 11 more flowers and leaves.

3. Place the 12 flower and leaf shapes on the 9-x-12-inch paper and glue them down in an orderly manner.

4. To make the chaotic design, provide students with construction paper scraps. They may cut out a variety of shapes and sizes, then glue the pieces onto 9-x-12-inch paper in a random manner.

The Fool of the World and the Flying Ship
Illustrated by Uri Shulevitz
Retold by Arthur Ransome
(New York: Farrar, 1968)
1969 Caldecott Award Winner

When the Czar proclaims that he will marry his daughter to the man who brings
him a flying ship, the Fool of the World sets out to try his luck and meets
some unusual companions along the way.

View from the Sky
From the sky the ground looks like a patchwork of color. Using pieces of construction paper the
students may make their own version of the ground. Details can be added with black marker or pen.

Art Concept: Aerial Perspective.
Looking at an object from above

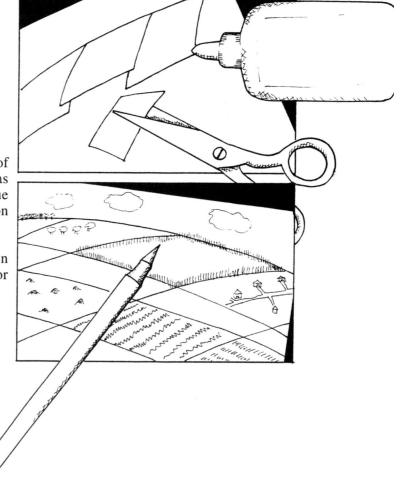

Materials.   Colored construction
            paper for the
            background
        Scraps of colored
            construction paper
        Markers or black pens
        Scissors
        Glue

Instructions.
1. Have the students cut out scraps of
    paper in the shape of the ground as
    it would appear from above. Glue
    these shapes onto the construction
    paper.

2. When all the pieces have been
    glued, add details with a marker or
    black pen.

Grandfather's Journey
By Allen Say
(Boston: Houghton Mifflin, 1993)
1994 Caldecott Award Winner

A Japanese American man recounts his grandfather's journey to America, which he later also undertakes, and the feelings of being torn by a love for two different countries.

Desert-Rock Collage

Examine the illustration in the story of the desert rocks. Notice how the warm color of the pink rock makes it dominate the picture and appear to come forward. The cool color of the blue rocks is not as bold. Using scraps of construction paper the students may make desert rocks.

Art Concepts:

Warm Colors. Colors that advance in a picture

Cool Colors. Color that recede in a picture

Materials. Scraps of colored
          construction paper
Background paper
Pencils
Scissors
Glue

Instructions.

1. Discuss warm and cool colors with students and ask them to select the colors they would like to use in their pictures. Instruct the students to begin tearing or cutting the scraps of colored construction paper into rock shapes. Ask the students to glue the shapes onto the background paper, keeping in mind the advancing and receding colors.

Grandfather's Journey
By Allen Say
(Boston: Houghton Mifflin, 1993)
1994 Caldecott Award Winner

A Japanese American man recounts his grandfather's journey to America, which he later also undertakes, and the feelings of being torn by a love for two different countries.

Torn-Paper Landscape

Look at the illustration in the story of the mountains. Notice how the shapes overlap to create depth. Using torn scrap construction paper, students may make a landscape that shows depth.

Art Concept: Depth. Created by overlapping shapes

Materials. Scraps of colored
    construction paper
    Background paper
    Glue

Instructions.

1. Ask students to tear scraps of construction paper into the shapes of mountains. Then overlap and glue the shapes to the background paper.

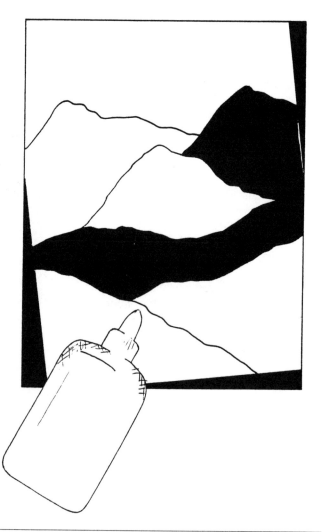

May I Bring a Friend?
Illustrated by Beni Montresor
Written by Beatrice Schenk de Regniers
(New York: Atheneum, 1964)
1965 Caldecott Award Winner

A young man is invited to visit the king and queen, and brings along his friends from the zoo.

Animal Shapes

Look at the animals throughout the book. Imagine how they would look without the black lines that give form to their flat shapes. Students may cut animal shapes out of colored construction paper and color the shapes with black crayon to achieve a look similar to the illustrations in the book.

__Art Concept: Form__. Shading may be added to a shape to give it a three-dimensional quality

__Materials__. Scraps of colored
                construction paper
        Background paper
        Black crayon
        Scissors
        Pencils
        Glue

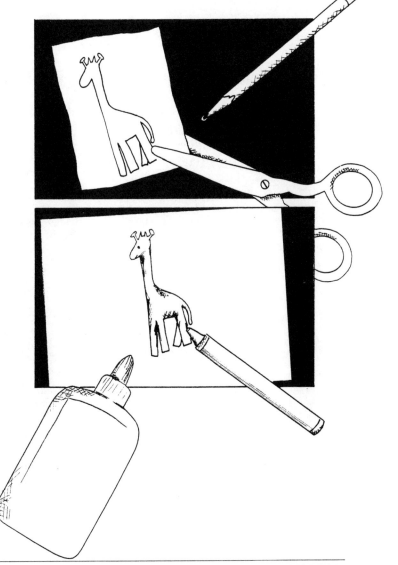

__Instructions__.

1. Ask the students to use a pencil to draw animal shapes on scrap paper. Cut out the shapes.

2. Instruct the students to glue the shapes onto background paper, then with black crayon add shaded areas to the shapes to give the flat shapes form.

Mei Li
Thomas Handforth
(New York: Doubleday, 1938)
1939 Caldecott Award Winner

A story about a little girl and her visit to the New Year's Day Fair.

Chinese Architecture

Notice the roof style on the buildings in the story. Using this element of Chinese architecture, students may make a building with colored construction paper.

Art Concept: Chinese Architecture. Roof style is a distinguishing element

Materials. Scraps of colored construction paper
Scissors
Glue
Background paper

Instructions.

1. Ask students to point out the differences between the buildings where they live and the buildings where Mei Li lives. Using scraps of construction paper, the students may make buildings using elements of Chinese architecture. Ask the students to cut the shapes needed and glue them onto the background paper.

Mirette on the High Wire
By Emily Arnold McCully
(New York: Putnam, 1992)
1993 Caldecott Award Winner

Mirette learns tightrope walking from Monsieur Bellini, a guest in her mother's
boarding house, not knowing that he is a celebrated tightrope artist
who has withdrawn from performing because of fear.

Shadow Collage

Mirette watches Bellini practicing through the window. His body casts a shadow on the side
of the building. Students can make a figure with a shadow using shapes cut from a magazine
and black construction paper.

Art Concept: Shadow. Dark area behind an image

Materials. Background paper
Black construction paper
Old magazines
Scissors
Pencils
Glue

Instructions.

1. Cut out a figure from an old magazine. Place the shape on black paper and trace the figure with a pencil. Cut out the black shape. Glue the black shape behind the cut out figure to create a shadow. Glue the figure and the shadow to the background paper.

Nine Days to Christmas
Illustrated by Marie Hall Ets
Written by Marie Hall Ets and Aurora Labastida
(New York: Viking, 1959)
1960 Caldecott Award Winner

A Mexican girl named Ceci chooses a special pinata for the Christmas celebration.

Newspaper Collage
Look at the illustration of the pinatas hanging outside of the factory in the story. Using newspaper the students can make a collage that shows unfinished pinatas hanging outside.

<u>Art Concept: Collage</u>. Design made by gluing pieces of paper to a surface

<u>Materials</u>.   Gray construction paper
Crayons
Newspaper
Glue
Scissors
Pencils

<u>Instructions</u>.
1. Have students draw the shapes of several animals on the newspaper using pencil, then cut out the shapes.

2. Glue the shapes onto the gray paper. Draw around the shapes with black crayon, and add the poles from which they would hang. Additional colors can be added with crayons.

Ox-Cart Man
Illustrated by Barbara Cooney
Written by Donald Hall
(New York: Viking, 1979)
1980 Caldecott Award Winner

The story depicts the yearly cycle of life for a New England farmer
during the nineteenth century.

Village Collage
The artist uses size to show the distance the ox-cart man has to travel on his journey. Some of the houses and trees are smaller than others, which gives the appearance of space. Have students make a landscape collage with different-size houses and trees.

Art Concept: Space. Objects in the distance appear smaller than those close to the viewer

Materials. Scraps of colored
construction paper
Background paper
Scissors
Crayons
Glue

Instructions.
1. Have students begin by drawing hills on the background paper with crayon.

2. Cut out a variety of sizes of small houses from the colored construction paper and glue them onto the hills, placing the smaller ones behind the larger houses. Add trees and other details with crayons.

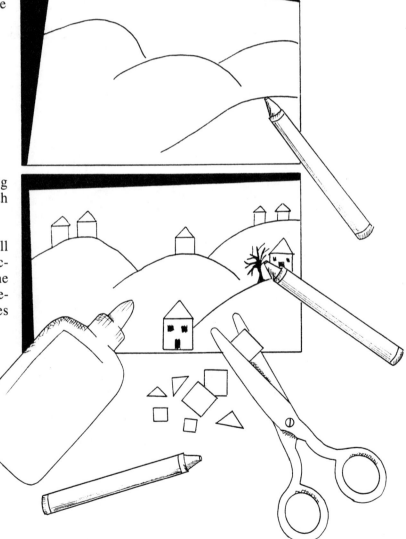

Prayer for a Child
Illustrated by Elizabeth Orton Jones
Written by Rachel Field
(New York: Macmillan, 1944)
1945 Caldecott Award Winner

This is a story about a child's bedtime prayer.

Face Collage

In the story the illustration that shows the faces of all the children uses the technique of overlapping to give the appearance of depth. Using faces cut from a magazine students may make a collage that shows depth.

Art Concept: Overlapping Shapes. Give the illusion of depth

Materials.　Background paper
Old magazines
Scissors
Glue

Instructions.

1.　Ask the students to cut out a number of faces from old magazines. Next ask them to glue the faces to the background paper so that they overlap.

Prayer for a Child
Illustrated by Elizabeth Orton Jones
Written by Rachel Field
(New York: Macmillan, 1944)
1945 Caldecott Award Winner

This is a story about a child's bedtime prayer.

Name Design

The artist begins each sentence with a large letter that looks three-dimensional because of the shading around the edges. Students may use this technique with the letters of their names.

Art Concept: Shading. Adding a darker area to give the object a three-dimensional look

Materials. 9-x-12-inch colored
          construction paper
12-x-18-inch colored
          construction paper
Scrap paper
Pencils
Scissors
Crayons
Glue

Instructions.
1. With pencil, have students lightly draw the first letter of their names using a single line on the 9-x-12-inch construction paper.

2. Fatten the letter by drawing around the shape, then cut out the letter.

3. Place the letter on top of a sheet of scrap paper. With the side of a peeled crayon ask students to trace around the edge of the shape. If the letter has a hole, such as a *p* or *o*, trace around the center.

4. Have students glue the letter to the larger paper and write the rest of their names with crayon.

Saint George and the Dragon
Illustrated by Trina Schart Hyman
Retold by Margaret Hodges
(Boston: Little, Brown, 1984)
1985 Caldecott Award Winner

Retells a segment from Spenser's *The Faerie Queen*, in which George, the Red Cross Knight,
slays the dreadful dragon that has been terrorizing the countryside for years,
thereby bringing peace and joy to the land.

Floral Panel
Using flowers as a theme, students can make a symmetrical panel similar to the ones that frame the illustrations in the story.

Art Concept: Symmetrical. The same on both sides of the central axis

Materials.   Scraps of colored
                    construction paper
                3-x-18-inch white paper
                Scissors
                Pencils
                Glue

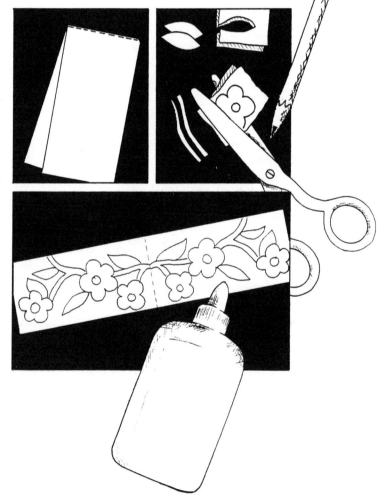

Instructions.
1. Ask the students to fold in half a 3-x-18-inch piece of paper.

2. Note that the students will need to cut two of every shape, so fold in half a scrap of paper and draw a flower or leaf shape on the paper. Cut the two pieces out at the same time.

3. Ask students to glue the pieces onto the 3-x-18-inch paper in the same spot on both sides of the center.

Shadow
Illustrated and translated by Marcia Brown
Written by Blaise Cendrars
(New York: Scribner, 1982)
1983 Caldecott Award Winner

Translated from the work by French poet Blaise Cendrars,
this story explores the mysterious world of shadows.

Face-and-Flame Collage

The illustration of the face at the end of the story uses an overlapping technique to create depth. Students may make a collage with tissue paper and construction paper.

<u>Art Concept: Space</u>. Overlapping of objects to create a sense of depth

<u>Materials</u>. Scraps of construction
              paper
              Black construction paper
              Background paper
              Tissue paper
              Scissors
              Glue

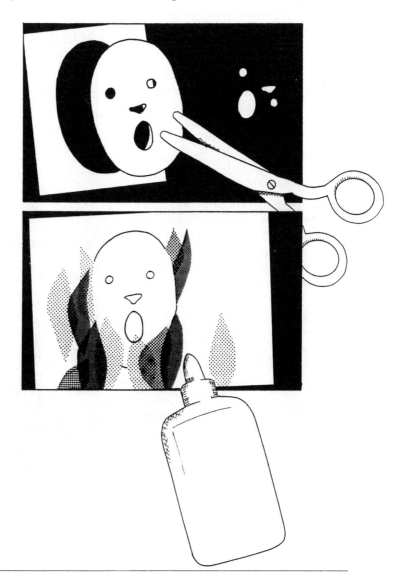

<u>Instructions</u>.
1. Using black paper have students cut out the shape of a face. Cut out holes for the eyes, nose, and mouth.

2. Cut out smoke and flame shapes from tissue paper and scraps of construction paper. Glue the face, flames, and smoke onto the construction paper, overlapping the pieces.

Shadow
Illustrated and translated by Marcia Brown
Written by Blaise Cendrars
(New York: Scribner, 1982)
1983 Caldecott Award Winner

Translated from the work by French poet Blaise Cendrars,
this story explores the mysterious world of shadows.

Shadow Design

Black shapes on bright backgrounds are used to draw the viewers' eyes to particular areas. Students may use construction paper to make a collage that uses this technique.

Art Concept: Emphasis. One part of a picture dominates to capture viewers' attention

Materials. Black construction paper
for figures
6-x-18-inch red
construction paper
6-x-18-inch orange
construction paper
12-x-18-inch
background paper
Scissors
Pencils
Glue

Instructions.
1. Using black construction paper have students lightly draw with pencil the outline of figures. Cut out the figures.

2. Have students tear the red and orange sheets of paper into long strips.

3. Glue the strips onto the background paper, then glue the black figures onto the orange and red design.

The Snowy Day
By Ezra Jack Keats
(New York: Viking, 1962)
1963 Caldecott Award Winner

The city where Peter lives is the setting for his day in the snow.

Cotton Collage
Look at the illustration of Peter playing on the snowy hill. Cotton balls pulled apart and glued to the surface of a piece of paper can give a similar look of wispy clouds.

Art Concept: Collage. Applying objects to a background paper to create a picture

Materials.   Blue construction paper
White construction paper
Scraps of construction
      paper
Cotton balls
Scissors
Pencils
Glue

Instructions.
1. Have students draw a hill shape on a piece of white paper with pencil. Then cut out the shape.

2. Glue the hill onto a piece of blue construction paper.

3. Using scraps of construction paper cut out figures playing in the snow and glue them onto the hill. Pull apart a cotton ball (so that it is thin) and glue it onto the paper over the hill and figures.

The Snowy Day
By Ezra Jack Keats
(New York: Viking, 1962)
1963 Caldecott Award Winner

The city where Peter lives is the setting for his day in the snow.

Simplified-Shape Collage

Throughout the book the artist uses simplified shapes to symbolize the different objects. Very little or no detail is used to represent such things as buildings and people. The students may create a collage in this same manner.

Art Concept: Shape. Simplified to create a picture

Materials. Scraps of colored
                construction paper
                Background paper
                Glue
                Scissors

Instructions.

1. Using scraps of colored construc-
    tion paper make a collage of a day
    out in the snow. Ask students to
    begin by cutting out shapes and
    gluing the pieces to background
    paper.

Tuesday
By David Wiesner
(New York: Clarion Books, 1991)
1992 Caldecott Award Winner

Frogs rise on their lily pads, float through the air, and explore
the nearby houses while the inhabitants sleep.

Flying Frogs

Notice how overlapping shapes in the illustrations create a sense of depth (e.g., small houses are placed behind the large frog shapes). Students may combine collage and drawing to create a picture that also gives the illusion of space.

Art Concept: Space. The illusion of depth through the use of different size objects

Materials.   Dark blue construction
            paper for the
            background
        Green construction paper
            for the frogs
        Crayons
        Glue
        Scissors
        Pencils

Instructions.

1. Demonstrate for students how to draw a frog by first drawing a circle very lightly with pencil.

2. Draw two circles on top for eyes, and add two small circles inside of the larger circles.

3. On the left side of the frog draw a *c* shape for a leg. On the right side draw a backward *c* for the other leg. Draw the frog's mouth.

4. To make the feet, connect three *v* shapes together.

5. Using green construction paper the students may imitate the above technique to draw three or four different-sized frogs. Cut the frogs out.

From *Art Through Children's Literature*. ©1994. Teacher Ideas Press, P.O. Box 6633, Englewood, CO 80155-6633, 1-800-237-6124.

6. With a pencil, draw the lily pads on scraps of paper. Cut them out, and glue the frogs to the pads.

7. Draw houses and trees on blue construction paper using crayons. The color of the crayons will appear dull on the dark paper, but this gives the appearance of nighttime. Glue the frogs on top of the crayon drawing.

Where the Wild Things Are
By Maurice Sendak
(New York: Harper & Row, 1963)
1964 Caldecott Award Winner

Max is sent to bed without his supper and dreams he is the king of the wild things.

Wild Thing

Notice the illustrations have lines repeated and overlapped to give the illusion of form to the flat shapes. Students may make their own creatures with shapes cut out of construction paper and with lines added with a fine-point marker or pen.

Art Concept: Illusion of Form. An object has a three-dimensional appearance

Materials. Scraps of colored
construction paper
Colored construction
paper for the
background
Fine-point markers or
pens
Scissors
Glue

Instructions.
1. Students can cut out shapes for their creatures using scraps of colored construction paper. Glue the shapes onto the background paper.

2. Using a pen or marker the students may add lines to the flat shape to give the appearance of form.

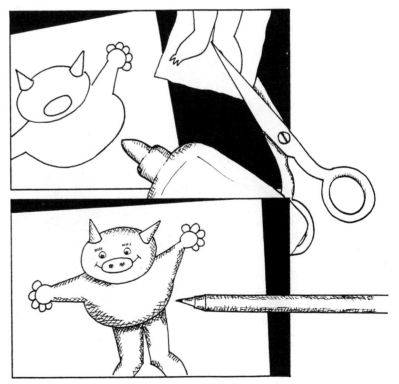

Why Mosquitoes Buzz in People's Ears
Illustrated by Leo and Diane Dillon
Retold by Verna Aardema
(New York: Dial, 1975)
1976 Caldecott Award Winner

A series of events occur as a result of a mosquito's exaggerated story.

Animal Collage
Examine the animals in the story and note how the animals appear as if they are made up of many smaller shapes. Using construction paper the students may make their own animal with qualities similar to those the artist used.

Art Concept: Collage. Making a picture by gluing smaller pieces of paper onto the surface of a larger sheet

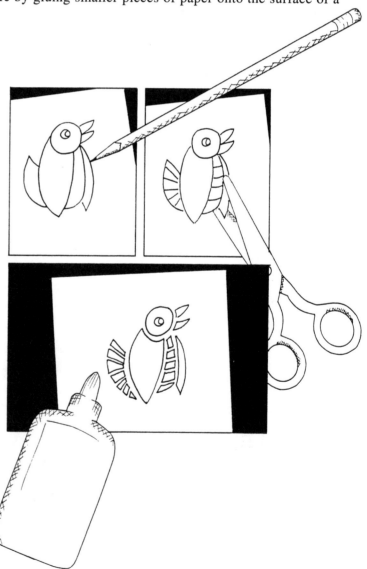

Materials. Colored construction
                paper for the
                background
                Scraps of colored
                construction paper
                Scissors
                Pencils
                Glue

Instructions.
1. Ask students to pick an animal they would like to make. Have them begin by drawing the shape of the animal with a pencil on the scrap paper. Then cut out the animal.

2. Using pencil divide the animal into smaller parts.

3. Cut the shapes apart, and glue the pieces to the background paper, leaving small spaces between the pieces.

Why Mosquitoes Buzz in People's Ears
Illustrated by Leo and Diane Dillon
Retold by Verna Aardema
(New York: Dial, 1975)
1976 Caldecott Award Winner

A series of events occur as a result of a mosquito's exaggerated story.

Pattern Snakes
The snake in the story is an example of pattern, because the design on the snake's body is repeated. Students may make a patterned snake using collage.

Art Concept: Pattern. Repetition of shapes

Materials. Colored construction
    paper for the
    background
Colored construction
    paper for the snake
Scissors
Pencils
Glue

Instructions.
1. Ask the students to draw the shape of a snake with pencil on a piece of construction paper. Suggest that a wider snake is easier to work with. Cut out and glue the snake onto a piece of construction paper.

2. Using scraps of paper the students may cut out a simple geometric shape. Copy the shape, and cut out enough to line the edge of the snake. Glue the shapes onto the snake. Cut out and glue smaller shapes onto the first shapes.

Chapter
8

Watercolors are water-soluble transparent colors. The lessons in this chapter focus on techniques such as dry brush painting, washes, using the white of the paper, and crayon resist.

Duffy and the Devil
Illustrated by Margot Zemach
Retold by Harve Zemach
(New York: Farrar, 1973)
1974 Caldecott Award Winner

A variation of the story Rumpelstiltskin with an unusual ending.

Watercolor Window

Notice the windows inside Squire Lovel's house and how the white of the paper is used to make the outline of the window. Using this method students may make a painting of a window.

<u>**Art Concept: Watercolor Technique**</u>. The white of the paper is used as a key element

<u>**Materials**</u>. Paper
Watercolor paint
Brushes
Water dishes

<u>**Instructions**</u>.

1. Ask the students to begin by painting the area around the window— the wall or curtains. Then paint the small areas of glass, leaving white between the sections.

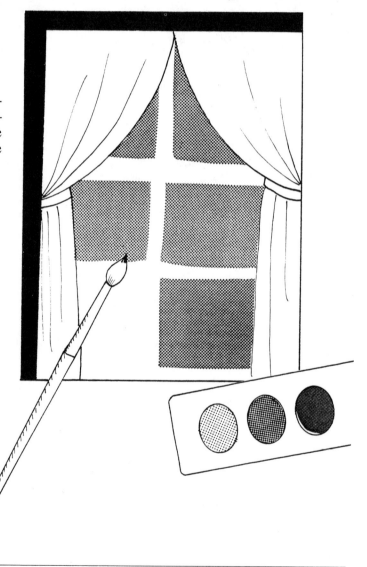

Fables
By Arnold Lobel
(New York: Harper & Row, 1980)
1981 Caldecott Award Winner

Twenty fables about an array of animal characters from
crocodile to ostrich, each containing a clever moral.

Candy Dream

Notice the technique the artist used to shade the objects in the illustrations. These shaded areas give flat objects a three-dimensional look. Examine the illustration of the pig in the fable "The Pig at the Candy Store." The pig loves candy so much that he dreams about it. Using the image of a pig, students may paint themselves in a dream with their favorite food. Shaded areas may be added with pencil over the watercolor painting.

Art Concept: Shade. Dark parts of a picture

Materials. Paper
Pencils
Watercolor paint
Water dishes
Brushes

Instructions.

1. With pencil, have students lightly draw a picture of themselves as a pig. Add food items, such as a pizza moon and pretzel stars, and paint the drawing with watercolors. Let the painting dry. Using pencil, students may add shaded areas.

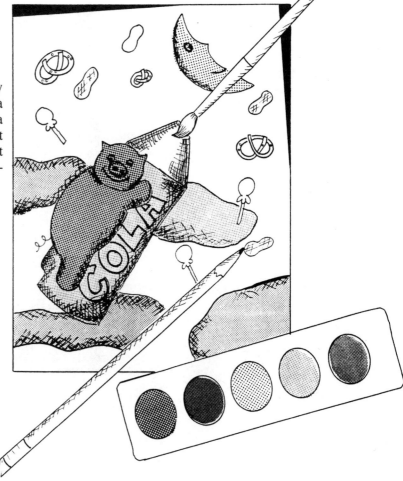

From *Art Through Children's Literature*. ©1994. Teacher Ideas Press, P.O. Box 6633, Englewood, CO 80155-6633, 1-800-237-6124.

The Funny Little Woman
Illustrated by Blair Lent
Retold by Arlene Mosel
(New York: Dutton, 1972)
1973 Caldecott Award Winner

A Japanese woman follows a rice dumpling into a hole in the ground
where she encounters a wicked Oni.

World of the Oni

In illustrations throughout the book, watercolor and line drawings are combined. The drawing is visible through the paint because of the transparent nature of watercolor paints. By combining pencil and watercolor paint, students may create their own idea of how the world of the Oni should look.

Art Concept: Transparency. The clear quality of watercolor paints

Materials. 	Paper
Pencils
Watercolor paint
Brushes
Water dish

Instructions.

1. Ask the students to draw with pencil their idea of what the world of the Oni should look like. When the drawing is complete, the students may add color using watercolor.

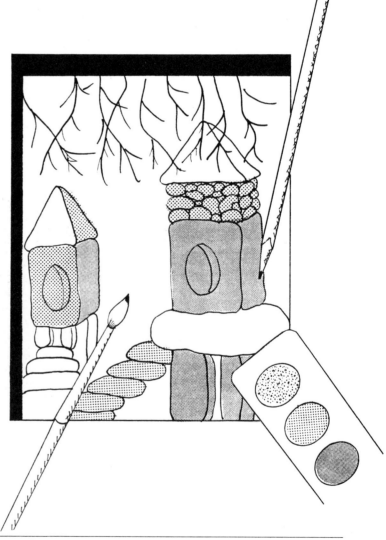

The Girl Who Loved Wild Horses
By Paul Goble
(New York: Bradbury Press, 1978)
1979 Caldecott Award Winner

Although she is fond of her people, a young girl prefers living among
wild horses where she is truly happy and free.

Moon over the Hills

Using the crayon-resist method, students may make a picture similar to the illustration of the moon over the hills.

Art Concept: Crayon-Resist. Paint does not adhere to that area of the paper where crayon has been used

Materials.   Black watercolor paint
Crayons
White paper
Brushes
Water dishes

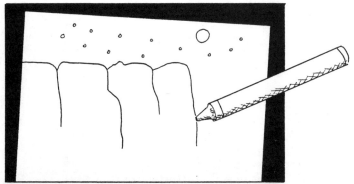

Instructions.

1. Ask the students to draw hills, stars, and the moon with light-colored crayons, but tell them the technique does not work if they apply the crayon lightly.

2. Have students coat the entire paper with black paint. The paint will not stick to the areas that have been drawn with crayon.

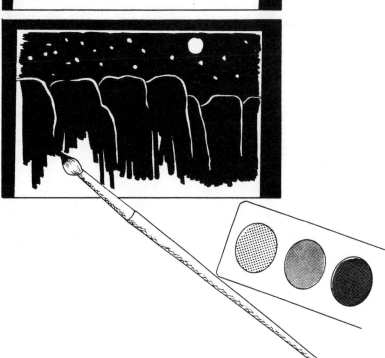

Many Moons
Illustrated by Louis Slobodkin
Written by James Thurber
(New York: Harcourt, Brace, 1943)
1944 Caldecott Award Winner

The King's staff attempts to fulfill a young princess' demand for the moon.

Castle with Fireworks

The Royal Mathematician came up with the idea of lighting fireworks every night to block Princess Lenore's view of the moon. To illustrate the fireworks, the artist used streaks of color. Students may combine crayon and paint to make their own version of how the castle would look with fireworks exploding in the background.

Art Concept: Paint and Crayon. Combined to make a picture

Materials. Paper
Crayons
Watercolor paint
Brushes
Water dishes

Instructions.

1. Have students draw the castle with crayon. Add streaks of color behind the castle with crayon and watercolor paints.

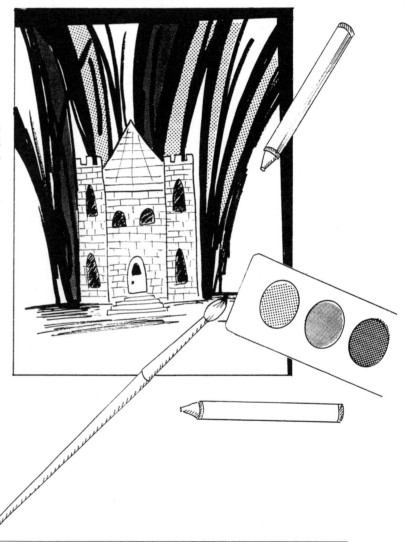

Many Moons
Illustrated by Louis Slobodkin
Written by James Thurber
(New York: Harcourt, Brace, 1943)
1944 Caldecott Award Winner

The King's staff attempts to fulfill a young princess' demand for the moon.

Moon Painting

Bold brush strokes are used throughout the illustrations in the book. Using large brush strokes students may paint a picture of the moon in the sky.

<u>Art Concept: Dry-Brush Painting</u>. More evident strokes are achieved by using only a small amount of water on the brush while painting

<u>Materials</u>.   Paper
Watercolor paint
Brushes
Water dishes

<u>Instructions</u>.

1. Have students draw the shape of the moon with pencil. Instruct the students to paint the sky and moon. Only a small amount of water is needed, because too much will cause the brush strokes to run together.

Mirette on the High Wire
By Emily Arnold McCully
(New York: Putnam, 1992)
1993 Caldecott Award Winner

Mirette learns tightrope walking from Monsieur Bellini, a guest in her mother's
boarding house, not knowing that he is a celebrated tightrope artist
who has withdrawn from performing because of fear.

Illuminated Light

Watercolor paintings use the white of the paper to add to the bright quality of the painting. The artist uses this technique throughout the book. Students may make a painting of a lamp or streetlight using this technique.

Art Concept: Watercolor Technique. White of the paper is used to add a bright quality to the painting.

Materials.   Watercolor paint
Paper
Brushes
Water dishes

Instructions.
1. Have students paint a picture of a lamp or post light, but keep the majority of the shape white. Add color to the background. The area near the light should have white showing through the color.

Mirette on the High Wire
By Emily Arnold McCully
(New York: Putnam, 1992)
1993 Caldecott Award Winner

Mirette learns tightrope walking from Monsieur Bellini, a guest in her mother's
boarding house, not knowing that he is a celebrated tightrope artist
who has withdrawn from performing because of fear.

Sky Painting

Mirette climbs onto the wire and attempts to walk across it. Notice the free quality the artist used to paint the sky. Students can paint a sky using the same technique.

Art Concept: Watercolor Paint. Characteristic of watercolor paint is the manner in which the transparent paint is freely applied

Materials.   Watercolor paint
Paper
Brushes
Water dishes

Instructions.

1. Provide students with several sheets of paper and ask them to experiment with a variety of colors. Test different quantities of water and paint on the brush. Remind them to leave some areas of the painting white just as the artist did.

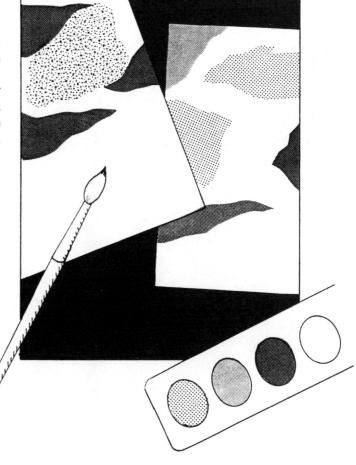

Noah's Ark
By Peter Spier
(New York: Doubleday, 1977)
1978 Caldecott Award Winner

Rhymes retell how pairs of every type of creature known climbed aboard
Noah's ark and survived the Flood.

Ark in the Rain

Examine the illustrations of the ark in the rain. Note that drawing and painting are combined to make the picture. Students can achieve a similar look by combining watercolor paints, crayon, and pencil.

Art Concept: Combining Media. Using several materials in one picture

Materials. Paper
Watercolor paint
Pencils
Crayons
Water dishes
Brushes

Instructions.

1. Using pencil have students draw an ark and water. Add additional details with the pencil, then paint the ark, sky, and water.

2. Give the picture time to dry. Using crayon draw streaks of rain to finish the drawing.

Noah's Ark
By Peter Spier
(New York: Doubleday, 1977)
1978 Caldecott Award Winner

Rhymes retell how pairs of every type of creature known climbed aboard
Noah's ark and survived the Flood.

Sequence of Events

To convey the effect of the rising water in the story, the artist places the ark higher and higher in the picture. Using watercolor paints and small panels students may illustrate this event.

Art Concept: Placement. Objects in the distance are placed higher on the paper

Materials. Paper
Watercolor paint
Pencils
Brushes
Water dishes

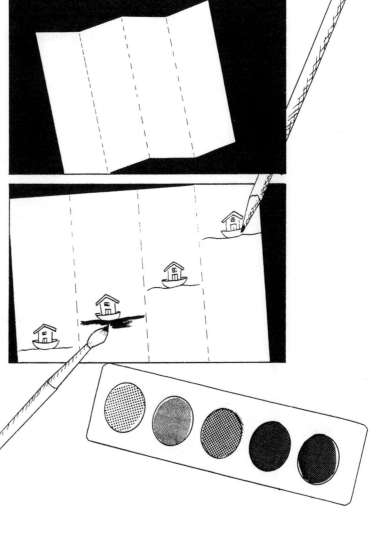

Instructions.
1. Divide the drawing paper into four or five rectangles.

2. Near the bottom of the paper draw with pencil the ark and the water level. Raise the level of the water in each drawing, placing the ark higher each time. Paint the picture using watercolors.

From *Art Through Children's Literature*. ©1994. Teacher Ideas Press, P.O. Box 6633, Englewood, CO 80155-5633, 1-800-237-6124.

Noah's Ark
By Peter Spier
(New York: Doubleday, 1977)
1978 Caldecott Award Winner

Rhymes retell how pairs of every type of creature known climbed aboard
Noah's ark and survived the Flood.

Sunset Painting

Look at the illustration of the bird taking a branch to Noah. The sun is setting in the background. Students may make a sunset painting using a wash technique.

<u>**Art Concept: Wash**</u>. Applying paint and gradually changing its value from light to dark

<u>**Materials**</u>.   Paper
                  Watercolor paint
                  Water dishes
                  Brushes
                  Pencils

<u>**Instructions**</u>.

1. Have students begin by drawing with pencil a line across the paper to divide the water and sky, then add the shape of the setting sun.

2. Select a color for the sky. First paint the sky with clear water, then starting at the top of the paper apply the paint and gradually dilute it with water, moving down the page.

3. Paint the sun and water.

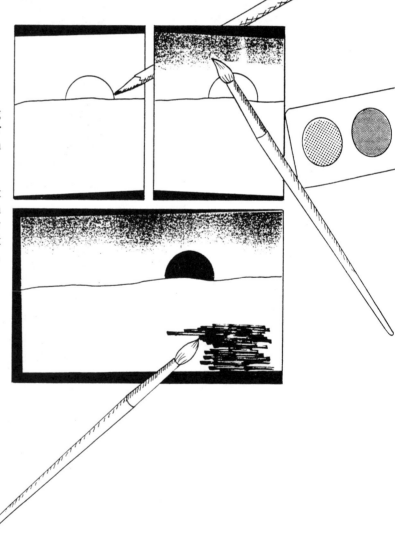

One Fine Day
Illustrated and retold by Nonny Hogrogian
(New York: Macmillan, 1971)
1972 Caldecott Award Winner

When a fox steals milk from a woman, she cuts off his tail to punish him.
He must return the milk before she will sew it back on.

Landscape Painting

Throughout the book the artist uses obvious brush strokes in the illustrations. A dry-brush technique may be used to make a picture with texture qualities similar to the textures in the story.

Art Concepts:

Texture. Surface quality of an object

Dry-brush Painting. Adding a small amount of paint to a brush that has been slightly moistened with water, then brushing the paint onto the paper so that the strokes are apparent

Materials.   Paper
                Watercolor paint
                Brushes
                Water dishes
                Pencils

Instructions.

1. Ask students to draw with pencil the ground and a few trees, then to place a small amount of paint on the brush. The brush should first be tested on a paper towel to ensure that there is not too much paint on it. Students should begin to paint using obvious brush strokes.

Owl Moon
Illustrated by John Schoenherr
Written by Jane Yolen
(New York: Philomel, 1987)
1988 Caldecott Award Winner

On a cold winter's night under a full moon, a father and daughter trek
into the woods to see the Great Horned Owl.

Moonlit Night Painting
To create a sky similar to the one painted on the cover of the book, students should use a technique called a wash. The moon can be made by blocking out a circle with white crayon so that the paint will not absorb into that area of the paper.

Art Concept: Wash. A technique used to cover a large area in a picture with paint

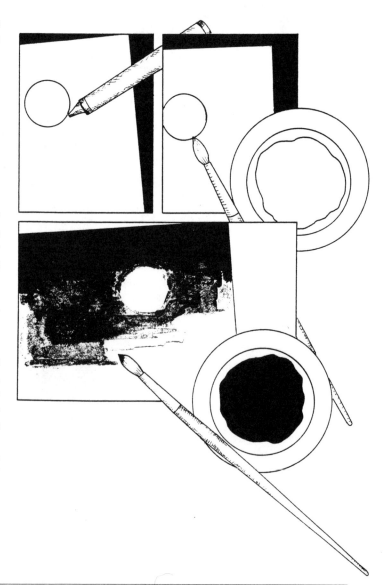

Materials.　White paper
　　　　　Watercolor paint
　　　　　Brushes
　　　　　Water dishes
　　　　　Pencils
　　　　　White crayons

Instructions.
1.　Have students draw on white paper with white crayon the shape of the moon. Color the moon shape in by pressing heavily to coat the paper's surface.

2.　Paint the surface of the white paper with water.

3.　Apply blue watercolor paint to the top part of the paper over the water, then instruct students to spread the paint across the paper and to decrease the amount of paint on the brush as they move down the page. The color at the bottom of the painting should fade to white. Lay the painting flat to dry.

Sylvester and the Magic Pebble
By William Steig
(New York: Simon & Schuster, 1969)
1970 Caldecott Award Winner

In a moment of fright, Sylvester the donkey asks his magic pebble to turn him into a
rock, but then cannot hold the pebble to wish himself back to normal again.

Crayon-Resist Sky

In the story Sylvester wishes for rain and a bolt of lightning fills the sky. Using the crayon-resist
technique students may paint a similarly stormy sky with watercolors.

Art Concept: Crayon-Resist. Drawing with crayon on a surface prohibits paint from soaking into
the paper in that area

Materials. White crayons
Paper
Watercolor paint
Brushes
Water dishes

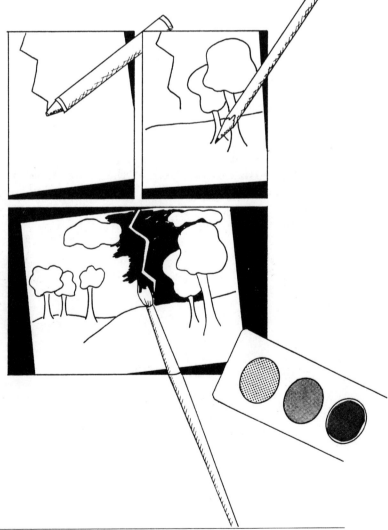

Instructions.
1. Have students draw with white
crayon a streak of lightning on their
paper.

2. Then draw the land and trees with
pencil.

3. When the drawing is complete, the
students may paint with watercolors. Point out that the crayon
resists the paint, so the lightning
bolt will show through.

From *Art Through Children's Literature*. ©1994. Teacher Ideas Press, P.O. Box 6633, Englewood, CO 80155-6633, 1-800-237-6124.

Time of Wonder
By Robert McCloskey
(New York: Viking, 1957)
1958 Caldecott Award Winner

Children explore the changing moods of an island.

Moon After the Storm

After the storm in the story the moon comes out and the bright color shines through the dark sky. Using a crayon-resist technique, students may make a similar picture.

Art Concept: Watercolor and Crayon-Resist. Crayon can be used to block out an area on a paper so that the paper does not absorb the watercolor paint

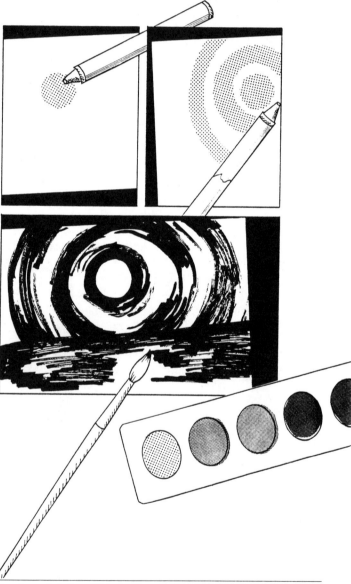

Materials. White paper
White crayons
Watercolor paint
Water dishes
Brushes

Instructions.

1. Have students draw a moon on the white paper using white crayon.

2. Using another white crayon from which the paper has been peeled, draw several wide bands around the moon with the flat part of the crayon.

3. Paint over the crayon with water-color paint.

Time of Wonder
By Robert McCloskey
(New York: Viking, 1957)
1958 Caldecott Award Winner

Children explore the changing moods of an island.

Morning Fog

In the story the sun begins to shine and the morning fog begins to lift in an effect that students may create by painting a yellow wash over a painting. To illustrate the fog, the intensity of the colors should be dulled by diluting the paint with water.

Art Concepts:

<u>Wash</u>. Diluted paint on paper

<u>Intensity</u>. Brightness or dullness of a color

<u>Materials</u>. White paper
Pencils
Watercolor paint
Water dishes
Brushes

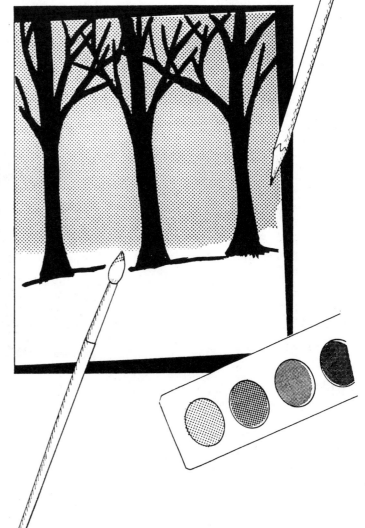

Instructions.

1. Ask students to lightly draw with pencil the outline of several trees, then paint the trees with diluted colors so that they are not too bright. After the painting dries, paint its entire surface with yellow paint that also has been watered-down.

Time of Wonder
By Robert McCloskey
(New York: Viking, 1957)
1958 Caldecott Award Winner

Children explore the changing moods of an island.

Watercolor Rain Painting

White crayon on white paper may be used to block out areas of the painting and give the appearance of rain. When paint is applied over the crayon, the crayon will resist the paint, not allowing it to absorb into the paper. Using this technique students may paint the drops of water in the rain.

Art Concept: Crayon-Resist. Crayon applied to the surface of paper stops paint from absorbing into the paper

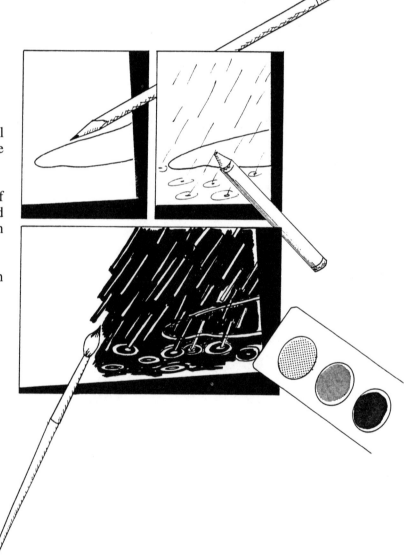

Materials. Pencils
White paper
White crayons
Watercolor paint
Water dishes

Instructions.

1. Ask students to outline with pencil the area of the paper where the ground is.

2. With white crayon draw streaks of rain pelting toward the ground and rings in the water and dots within those rings where the rain hits.

3. Then paint over the crayon with green and blue watercolors.

Chapter

9

Tempera paints are water-soluble paints with an opaque quality. The tempera chapter explores traditional methods of applying paint with a brush and nontraditional tools such as sponges, old toothbrushes, cotton swabs, and crumpled paper. Lessons also include painting over crayon surfaces to create etchings and applying crayon to the top of dried paint to add details.

Always Room for One More
Illustrated by Nonny Hogrogian
Written by Sorche Nic Leodhas, pseud. [Leclaire Alger]
(New York: Holt, Rinehart & Winston, 1965)
1966 Caldecott Award Winner

A kind man invites passersby into his small home. Based upon the
Scottish ballad of the same title.

Sponge Painting

Paintings are not always made with traditional tools such as paintbrushes. Sponge dipped in paint and stamped onto a paper gives a look similar to what the artist achieved for the book.

Art Concept: Sponge. Used as a tool for painting

Materials.　Colored construction
　　　　　　　paper
　　　　　　Paint
　　　　　　Small sponges
　　　　　　Paint dishes
　　　　　　Black markers
　　　　　　Newspaper

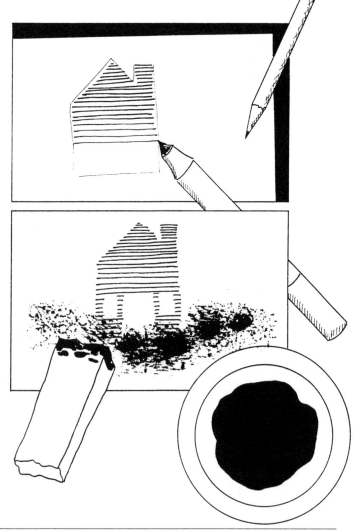

Instructions.

1.　Direct students to lightly sketch with pencil the outline of a house, then with a marker draw lines to complete the house.

2.　Place the drawing on top of a sheet of newspaper, then pour a small amount of paint in the bottom of a paint dish. Dab the sponge into the paint and begin stamping it gently onto the paper until the sponge no longer has paint on it. Repeat the above steps with a second color.

Always Room for One More
Illustrated by Nonny Hogrogian
Written by Sorche Nic Leodhas, pseud. [Leclaire Alger]
(New York: Holt, Rinehart & Winston, 1965)
1966 Caldecott Award Winner

A kind man invites passersby into his small home. Based upon the
Scottish ballad of the same title.

Value Painting
Paint applied with a crumpled piece of paper can be used to achieve areas of light and dark. Using this technique students can create similar illustrations to those made by the original artist.

<u>Art Concept: Value</u>. The lightness and darkness of a color

<u>Materials</u>.   Paper
               Paint
               Scrap paper for
                     crumpling
               Paint dishes
               Newspaper

<u>Instructions</u>.
1. Have students place a piece of paper on top of a sheet of newspaper. Crumple a piece of scrap paper, place a small amount of paint in a dish, and dip the crumpled paper into the paint. Stamp it gently onto the paper. Repeat the above steps with another color.

The Biggest Bear
By Lynd Ward
(Boston: Houghton Mifflin, 1952)
1953 Caldecott Award Winner

When Johnny goes hunting for a bear, he instead returns with a live cub.
As the cub grows problems begin.

Scratch-Art Bear

Notice how the small lines on the bear in the story's illustrations are used to indicate the texture of the animal's fur. Using the technique of scratch art students may make a bear drawing that shows texture.

Art Concepts:

Scratch Art. Technique of placing a coating of paint on top of a paper that has been coated with crayon and making a design by scratching away areas of dried paint with a pointed tool

Texture. Surface quality of an object

Materials. Heavy drawing paper
White crayons
Brown paint
Brushes
Paper clips

Instructions.

1. Using white crayon, students cover the entire surface of their drawing paper, pressing hard so that the paper does not show through. The technique will not work if the crayon is applied too lightly. If white paper is used, it is difficult to tell where it has been colored, so manila paper works best if it is available.

2. Then coat the surface of the crayon-colored paper with several coats of brown paint. Let the paint dry.

3. Using an opened paper clip students may scratch a drawing of a bear into the surface of the paint.

The Biggest Bear
By Lynd Ward
(Boston: Houghton Mifflin, 1952)
1953 Caldecott Award Winner

When Johnny goes hunting for a bear, he instead returns with a live cub.
As the cub grows problems begin.

Sponge Trees

Look carefully at the trees in the illustration of the bear pulling Johnny toward the little log house. To obtain a look similar to the one in the picture, students may use a sponge to paint trees.

Art Concept: Sponge. Used as a tool for painting

Materials. Paper
Brown and white paint
Sponges
Paint dishes
Brushes

Instructions.

1. Have students begin by mixing a small amount of brown paint into white paint. Using a brush, paint the tree trunk.

2. Add paint to the center of the tree top to achieve the impression of branches and leaves. Gradually work the sponge toward the outer edge as the amount of paint on the sponge decreases.

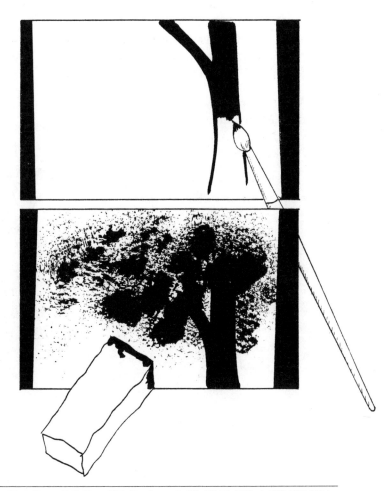

Chanticleer and the Fox
Illustrated and adapted by Barbara Cooney
(New York: Thomas Y. Crowell, 1958)
1959 Caldecott Award Winner

A tale of a sly fox and a rooster.

Leaves with Shadows

Examine the leaves and acorns at the end of the story and notice how form is added to the flat green shapes by including areas of black. Using black marker over areas of paint the students may make leaves with a similar quality.

Art Concept: Shadow. Added to a flat shape to give an object form

Materials.   Paper
Pencils
Green paint
Brushes
Markers

Instructions.
1. Ask students to use a pencil to draw leaves and acorns, then paint these shapes with green paint.

2. When the paint has dried, add areas of black with a marker.

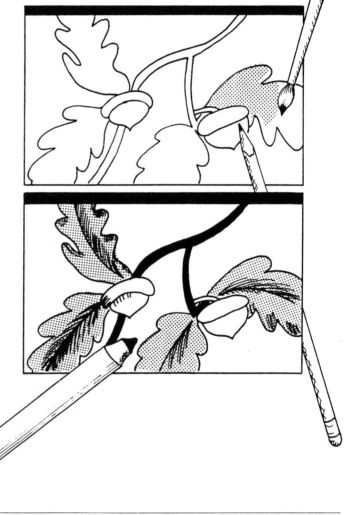

Chanticleer and the Fox
Illustrated and adapted by Barbara Cooney
(New York: Thomas Y. Crowell, 1958)
1959 Caldecott Award Winner

A tale of a sly fox and a rooster.

Thatched Cottage

Note the style of cottage in which the story's widow and her daughters live—especially its thatched roof. The artist uses repeating lines to give the sense of the roof's texture. Using crayon on top of dried paint, students may make their own thatched-roof cottage.

Art Concept: Line. Repeated to show texture

Materials.   Paper
Pencils
Paint
Brushes
Crayons

Instructions.
1. Ask students to draw with pencil the shape of a cottage and paint the drawing with tempera paint.

2. When the painting is dry, add details on top of the painting with crayons.

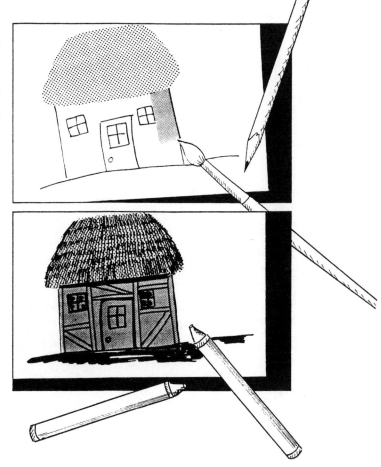

Chanticleer and the Fox
Illustrated and adapted by Barbara Cooney
(New York: Thomas Y. Crowell, 1958)
1959 Caldecott Award Winner

A tale of a sly fox and a rooster.

White-Crayon Etching

Note in the story the illustrations of the grass hills and the sky. The white of the paper shows through the shapes as if the color were scratched away. Students may make a similar landscape picture using the etching technique.

Art Concept: Etching. Using a sharp tool to scratch into a surface

Materials. White paper
White crayons
Blue and green paint
Brushes
Paper clips

Instructions.
1. Direct students to color heavily on the white paper with a white crayon. Cover the entire surface.

2. Using green and blue paint the students should then paint the sky and grass. This may take a few coats, because the crayon will resist the paint. Let the paint dry.

3. With an opened paper clip, scratch into the green and blue to expose the white underneath.

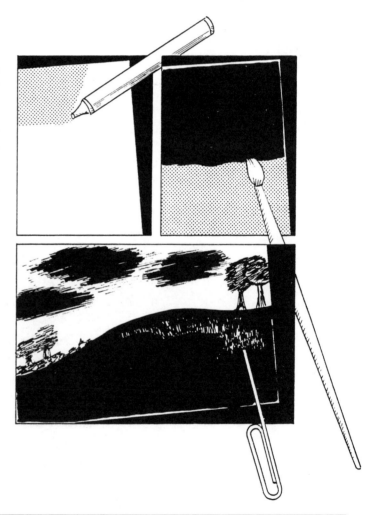

Drummer Hoff
Illustrated by Ed Emberley
Written by Barbara Emberley
(Englewood Cliffs, N.J.: Prentice-Hall, 1967)
1968 Caldecott Award Winner

A story told in verse about the assembling and firing of a cannon.

Soldier Painting

For the faces of the characters in the story, contour lines are used to make the simplified shapes. Using paint and crayons, students may make their own character using simplified features.

Art Concept: Contour Lines. Outline of an object

Materials.　Paper
　　　　　　　Pencils
　　　　　　　Paint
　　　　　　　Brushes
　　　　　　　Crayons

Instructions.
1.　Have students draw the face of a soldier with pencil, then add color with paint.

2.　When the paint is dry, have students outline the shapes with black crayon.

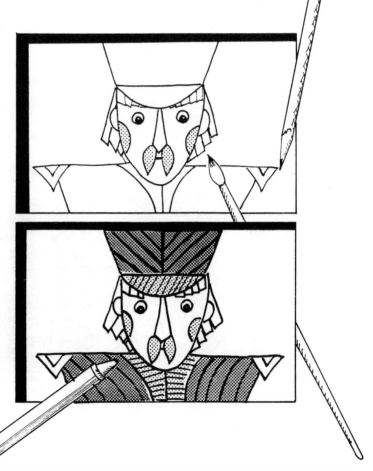

Finders Keepers
Illustrated by Nicolas [Nicolas Mordvinoff]
Written by Will [William Lipkind]
(New York: Harcourt, Brace, 1951)
1952 Caldecott Award Winner

Two dogs find a bone and learn a lesson about sharing.

Scratch-Art Design

Examine the illustration on the title page and note how the black looks almost as if it were scratched away to reveal the white, red, and yellow underneath. Scratch art is a technique that gives a result similar to the one the artist achieved. Students may write their names using this technique.

Art Concept: Scratch-Art Technique. Process of coloring the surface of a paper with crayon, then coating the surface with paint and scratching a design into the dried paint to expose the color below

Materials.   Paper
Crayons
Black paint
Brushes
Paper clips

Instructions.

1. Direct students to cover the entire surface of the drawing paper with crayon. Press hard enough so that the paper does not show through. The technique will not work if the crayon is too light.

2. Coat the surface of the crayon with paint—possibly with several coats to cover the surface completely. Let the paint dry.

3. Using the end of an opened paper clip, have students scratch their names into the paint.

The Glorious Flight:
Across the Channel with Louis Blériot
By Alice and Martin Provensen
(New York: Viking, 1983)
1984 Caldecott Award Winner

A biography of the man whose fascination with flying machines produced the Blériot XI,
which crossed the English Channel in thirty-seven minutes in the early 1900s.

Airplane Painting

Through color the artist conveys that the story takes place in the early 1900s. Students can achieve a similar look by painting on brown paper with thinned paint.

Art Concept: Tempera Paint. A paint with an opaque quality that, when watered down, can be used as a transparent paint through which the color of the paper shows

<u>Materials</u>.   Brown construction paper
Paint
Brushes
Pencils

<u>Instructions</u>.
1. Ask students to draw an airplane on the paper with pencil. Using paint that has been thinned with water, students may paint the airplane and sky.

The Little Island
Illustrated by Leonard Weisgard
Written by Golden MacDonald, pseud. [Margaret Wise Brown]
(New York: Doubleday, 1946)
1947 Caldecott Award Winner

The little island changes along with the seasons.

Stormy Sea

Examine the illustration of the island during the storm and note how the waves are painted. To convey the mood of a storm, students should paint using bold strokes.

Art Concept: Mood. Conveyed through the use of brush strokes

Materials. Paper
Paint
Brushes

Instructions.

1. Ask students to paint a picture of the island in the story as they imagine it would look during a storm. Use bold strokes to convey the mood.

Madeline's Rescue
By Ludwig Bemelmans
(New York: Viking, 1953)
1954 Caldecott Award Winner

Madeline is rescued from drowning by a dog.

Night Painting

To illustrate the story's dark rooms the artist uses bold black strokes over the picture. Using black paint and crayon in this way, students may make a picture of one of the story's characters turning on the light.

Art Concept: Strokes. Their use can be an expressive element

Materials.   Yellow paper
Pencils
Crayons
Black paint
Brushes

Instructions.

1. Ask students to draw with pencil one of the girls or Miss Clavel in her bed turning on the light. Add color using crayons. With black paint, cover the areas of the paper around the figure with large strokes.

Once a Mouse
Illustrated and retold by Marcia Brown
(New York: Scribner, 1961)
1962 Caldecott Award Winner

A fable from India about a mouse who is rescued by a hermit.

Hiding in the Trees

At first glance the trees in the story appear to be just trees, but if you look carefully you can see animals painted in some of the trees that you might overlook with a quick glance. Students may paint a silhouette of a tree with different shapes hidden in the branches.

Art Concept: Silhouette. Picture made in a single color

Materials.   Pencils
Paper
Black paint
Brushes

Instructions.

1. Using a pencil, have students draw the shape of a tree. Begin with the trunk, then draw the wide branches, then the smaller branches. Add a few animals on the branches of the tree, but paint the tree and the animals with one color.

One Fine Day
Illustrated and retold by Nonny Hogrogian
(New York: Macmillan, 1971)
1972 Caldecott Award Winner

When a fox steals milk from a woman, she cuts off his tail to punish him.
He must return the milk before she will sew it back on.

Forest Painting with Sponge

Notice how the artist shows the texture of the trees in the illustrations. Students may use a sponge to paint a forest with texture.

Art Concept: Texture. Surface quality of an object

Materials. Paper
Paint
Sponge pieces
Paint dishes

Instructions.

1. Place a small amount of paint in the bottom of a paint dish. Ask students to dip only the end of a sponge in the paint. Begin by using long strokes to paint the trunks, then add color to the background and the treetops using smaller strokes.

Ox-Cart Man
Illustrated by Barbara Cooney
Written by Donald Hall
(New York: Viking, 1979)
1980 Caldecott Award Winner

The story depicts the yearly cycle of life of a New England farmer
during the nineteenth century.

Cotton-Swab Painting

Examine the illustration in the story of the apple blossoms in May and note how the tree's blooms
are made up of small dots of pinks and white. Students may paint an apple tree in bloom using similar
colors and a cotton swab.

Art Concept: Painting Tools. Cotton swabs may be used to apply paint

Materials. Paper
Pencils
Paint
Brushes
Cotton swabs

Instructions.

1. Have students begin by drawing
with a pencil the shape of a tree
trunk and branches. Paint the tree
and the background using a paintbrush.

2. Let the painting dry. Using a cotton
swab, begin dabbing dots of paint
over the tree to make leaves.

The Rooster Crows
By Maud and Miska Petersham
(New York: Macmillan, 1945)
1946 Caldecott Award Winner

A collection of rhymes and chants.

Cloud Design

Examine the sky illustrations throughout the book and notice that some are made with tiny dots. Using a spatter technique students may create a cloud design.

Art Concept: Spattered-Picture Technique. A toothbrush dipped in paint and brushed over a pencil may be used to spray a piece of paper on which cut out scraps of paper have been placed

Materials.   Old toothbrushes
Paper
Scraps for making clouds
Paint
Newspaper
Scissors

Instructions.

1. Using the scraps of paper, have students cut out cloud shapes and place them on top of a sheet of paper.

2. Dip an old toothbrush into paint, and hold it close to the paper. Rub the bristles across a pencil. Dots of paint will appear on the paper.

3. To avoid smudging the dots, wait until the paint is dry to remove the cut out cloud shapes.

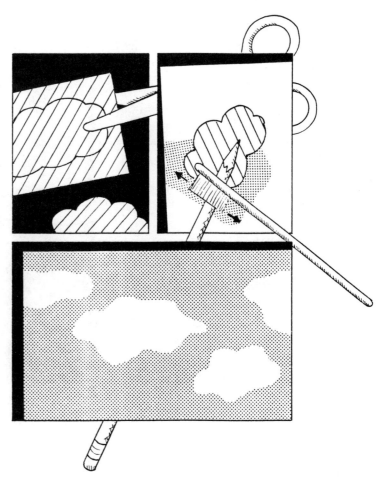

From *Art Through Children's Literature*. ©1994. Teacher Ideas Press, P.O. Box 6633, Englewood, CO 80155-6633, 1-800-237-6124.

A Tree Is Nice
Illustrated by Marc Simont
Written by Janice Udry
(New York: Harper & Row, 1956)
1957 Caldecott Award Winner

Trees and their many characteristics are described during different seasons.

Tree Painting with Warm Colors

Warm colors—red, orange, and yellow—are used in the story's illustration of the trees in the fall. Students may use these colors and a sponge to paint a picture of trees.

Art Concept: Warm Colors. Red, yellow, and orange

Materials.   Paper
Paint
Brushes
Sponge pieces
Paint dishes

Instructions.

1. Using brown paint, have students paint the trunks of the trees with a brush.

2. With a sponge, stamp the tops of the trees with red, orange, and yellow paint to create the look of leaves.

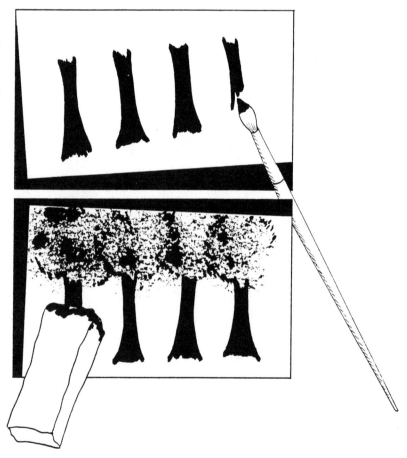

White Snow, Bright Snow
Illustrated by Roger Duvoisin
Written by Alvin Tresselt
(New York: Lothrop, Lee & Shepard, 1947)
1948 Caldecott Award Winner

A snowfall shows the difference in reactions between children and adults.

Snowy Night

To give the appearance of a snowy night, students may paint a picture on black construction paper. The size of the objects can be controlled to show space.

Art Concept: Space. Large objects placed in the foreground and small objects placed in the background give the appearance of depth

<u>Materials</u>. Black construction paper
Paint
Brushes
Pencils

<u>Instructions</u>.
1. Ask the students to decide what items they are going to put in their painting, then have them draw their picture with pencil on the black construction paper. Shapes in the distance should be drawn smaller than shapes close up.

2. Begin the painting by adding color to the shapes. Paint white dots for the falling snow last.

From *Art Through Children's Literature*. ©1994. Teacher Ideas Press, P.O. Box 6633, Englewood, CO 80155-6633, 1-800-237-6124.

Chapter

10

The focus of this chapter is color mixing. When mixing colors to create new colors, artists use the color wheel for its logical arrangement of colors. The primary colors are red, yellow, and blue. By mixing the primaries together in equal parts, secondary colors—orange, purple, and green—may be made. Intermediate colors are made when two primary colors are mixed together in unequal parts. Red orange is made when there is a larger amount of red than yellow, and yellow orange is made when there is a larger amount of yellow than red. Tints, shades, and tones can be made by adding white, black, and gray or the complement to the colors. You may want to examine the colors of the color wheel in the introduction and compare them to the colors in many of the Caldecott books. Note that the books use many more colors than appear on the color wheel. This chapter provides lessons which focus on mixing colors to create new colors.

Arrow to the Sun
By Gerald McDermott
(New York: Viking, 1974)
1975 Caldecott Award Winner

A Pueblo legend about an Indian boy's search for his father, the Sun.

Monochromatic Design

Throughout the book the artist uses shades of orange in the illustrations. Students may paint a design using shades of orange.

Art Concept: Monochromatic Color. Light and dark shades of a single color

Materials.   Pencils
Orange, black, and white
paint
White paper
Brushes
Paint dishes

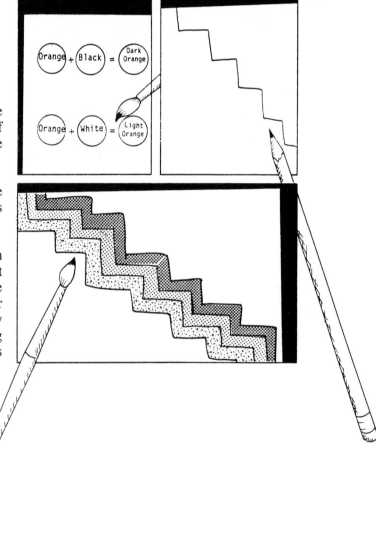

Instructions.

1. Demonstrate mixing colors for the class by adding small amounts of black or white paint to the pure color orange.

2. Ask students to draw a line on the paper with pencil that moves across the paper similar to steps.

3. Have students paint the line with orange paint. Mix a small amount of white or black paint with the orange, and paint a line on either side of the first line with the new color. Repeat mixing and painting different shades until the paper is covered.

The Biggest Bear
By Lynd Ward
(Boston: Houghton Mifflin, 1952)
1953 Caldecott Award Winner

When Johnny goes hunting for a bear, he instead returns with a live cub.
As the cub grows problems begin.

Barn Painting

To give the buildings three-dimensional form, the artist paints the picture with light and dark areas. Using tints and shades of the color brown, students may paint a barn or house.

Art Concepts:

Tints. Color plus white

Shade. Color plus black

Materials.   Paper
Brown, white, and black
paint
Pencils
Brushes
Paint dishes

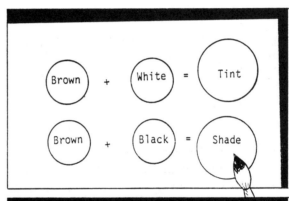

Instructions.

1. Demonstrate for the class how to make tints and shades of brown. Begin with brown and add small amounts of black or white to slowly change the color.

2. Ask students to draw the shape of a barn or a house with pencil. Then instruct them to mix black or white to the brown and begin painting.

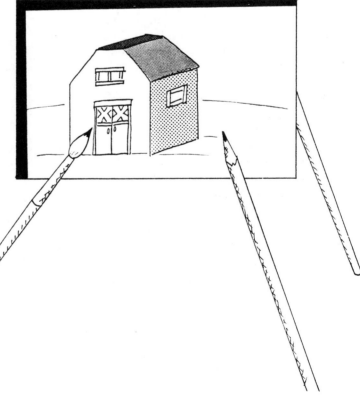

From *Art Through Children's Literature*. ©1994. Teacher Ideas Press, P.O. Box 6633, Englewood, CO 80155-6633, 1-800-237-6124.

The Egg Tree
By Katherine Milhous
(New York: Scribner, 1950)
1951 Caldecott Award Winner

A family tradition of egg decorating is passed on.

Complementary Color Mixing

The colors used throughout the book are dulled. Students can paint an egg tree using the same type of colors. Dulled colors can be made by mixing a color with a small amount of its complement.

Art Concepts:

Complementary Colors. Opposite on the color wheel

Complementary Color Mixing. When a color is mixed with a small amount of its complement, the color is dulled

Materials. Paper
Paint
Pencils
Brushes
Paint dishes

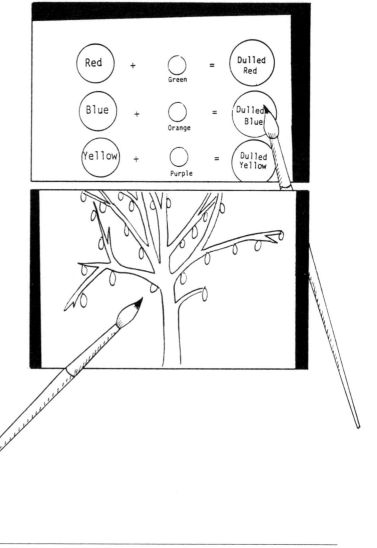

Instructions.

1. Discuss complementary colors with the class, and demonstrate how a primary color such as red is dulled with a drop of its complement, green.

2. Instruct the students to paint an egg tree using dulled colors.

The Little Island
Illustrated by Leonard Weisgard
Written by Golden MacDonald, pseud. [Margaret Wise Brown]
(New York: Doubleday, 1946)
1947 Caldecott Award Winner

The little island changes along with the seasons.

Fish Under the Sea

To illustrate how fish look under the sea the artist uses shades of green. Students may paint an underwater scene with monochromatic colors.

Art Concept: Monochromatic. Color plus white or black

Materials.   Green, black, and white
paint
Paper
Pencils
Paint dishes
Brushes

Instructions.

1. Demonstrate for the class how to make shades of green by adding small amounts of black or white to the pure color. Ask students to draw fish and plants with pencil and paint using shades of green.

2. After the picture has dried, have students paint over the shapes with watered-down shades of green.

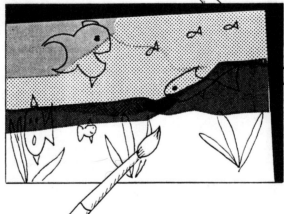

The Little Island
Illustrated by Leonard Weisgard
Written by Golden MacDonald, pseud. [Margaret Wise Brown]
(New York: Doubleday, 1946)
1947 Caldecott Award Winner

The little island changes along with the seasons.

Moonlit Night

In the story, examine the illustration of the boats sailing to the little island. The artist uses shades of blue to illustrate the scene. The students should also use shades of blue to paint a picture of boats in the moonlit night.

Art Concept: Monochromatic.
Light and dark shades of a single color

Materials. Blue, black, and white paint
Pencils
Paper
Brushes
Paint dishes

Instructions.
1. Demonstrate mixing colors for the students. Begin by adding small amounts of white or black to the pure color blue.

2. Using pencil students may draw a picture of boats nearing the little island. Paint the drawing with shades of blue.

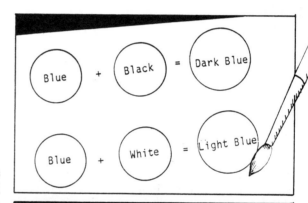

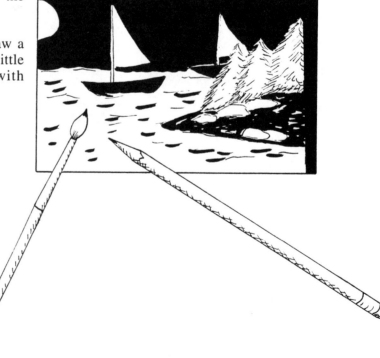

Many Moons
Illustrated by Louis Slobodkin
Written by James Thurber
(New York: Harcourt, Brace, 1943)
1944 Caldecott Award Winner

The King's staff attempts to fulfill a young princess' demand for the moon.

Castle Painting

The picture of the castle at the beginning of the story is painted with the soft tints of blue and pink. Even the trees are painted with the same colors, which gives the castle a peaceful look. Using the same colors students may paint a castle.

Art Concept: Tint. Color plus white

Materials. Paper
Pencils
Paint
Brushes
Paint dishes

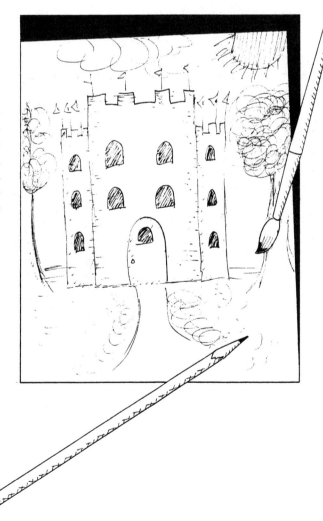

Instructions.

1. Demonstrate mixing tints for students by adding white to the pure colors blue and red. Ask students to begin by drawing, with pencil, a picture of the castle and the area around the castle. Have them complete their picture with tints of blue and red.

Song of the Swallows
By Leo Politi
(New York: Scribner, 1949)
1950 Caldecott Award Winner

The gardener of a church in San Juan tells a young boy a story about swallows.

Flowers

Notice how the artist uses the color pink throughout the book. Pink is a tint made by mixing white and red. Students may paint flowers using the color pink.

Art Concept: Tint. Color plus white

Materials. Red and white paint
Paint dishes
Brushes
Pencils
Paper

Instructions.
1. Demonstrate mixing red and white together for the students.

2. Ask students to begin by drawing flowers with pencil. Add color using tints of red.

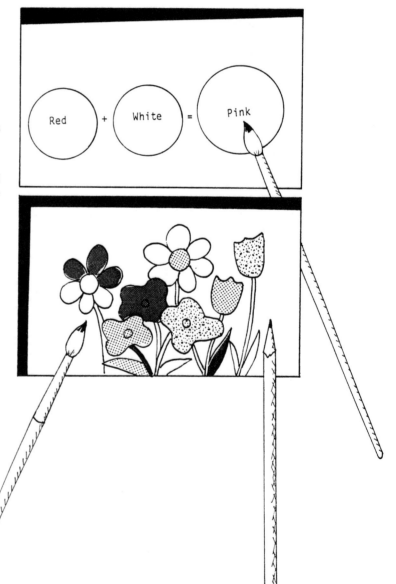

Song of the Swallows
By Leo Politi
(New York: Scribner, 1949)
1950 Caldecott Award Winner

The gardener of a church in San Juan tells a young boy a story about swallows.

Swallow Painting

Examine the illustration of the swallows returning to Juan's home to nest. Students may make a painting of the swallows using similar colors.

Art Concepts:

Tint. Color plus white

Shade. Color plus black

Materials. Red, black, and white paint
Paper
Brushes
Pencils
Paint dishes

Instructions.

1. Demonstrate mixing tints and shades for students. Mix small amounts of white or black to red, gradually changing the color.

2. Instruct the students to draw the swallows and a background with pencil. Using tints and shades students may add color to the drawing.

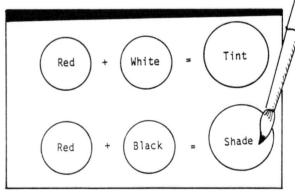

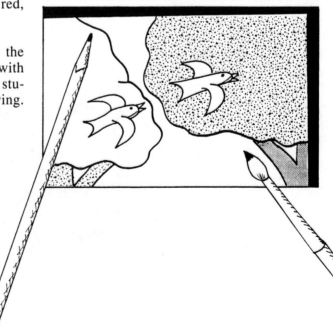

From *Art Through Children's Literature*. ©1994. Teacher Ideas Press, P.O. Box 6633, Englewood, CO 80155-6633, 1-800-237-6124.

A Tree Is Nice
Illustrated by Marc Simont
Written by Janice Udry
(New York: Harper & Row, 1956)
1957 Caldecott Award Winner

Trees and their many characteristics are described during different seasons.

Tree Painting

The color yellow green, which the artist uses in the illustration of the woods, is an intermediate color. Green is a secondary color. By mixing the primary colors blue and yellow, students may make secondary and intermediate colors. The various shades of green may be used to paint a picture of the woods, and details may be added with crayon.

Art Concepts:

Primary Colors. Red, yellow, and blue

Secondary Colors. Orange, violet, and green

Intermediate Colors. Yellow orange, yellow green, blue green, blue violet, red violet, and red orange

Materials.   Blue and yellow paint
Paper
Brushes
Paint dishes
Crayons

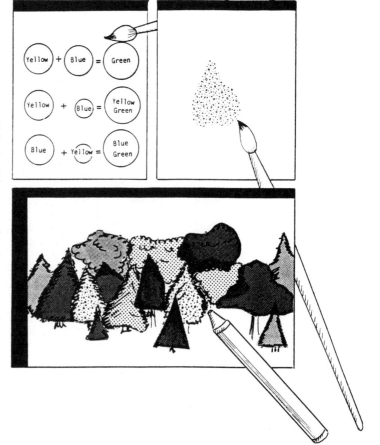

Instructions.

1.   Demonstrate mixing the color green for the students by stirring together equal amounts of blue and yellow paint. Vary the amounts of blue and yellow to make shades of yellow green and blue green.

2.   Instruct students to begin their painting using colors mixed from yellow and blue.

3.   Let the painting dry completely. Use crayon add details to the trees, such as trunks and leaves.

A Tree Is Nice
Illustrated by Marc Simont
Written by Janice Udry
(New York: Harper & Row, 1956)
1957 Caldecott Award Winner

Trees and their many characteristics are described during different seasons.

Winter Day Painting

Orange, purple, and green are secondary colors that are the main colors used in the picture of the house and tree on the winter day. Students may make secondary colors needed for the painting by mixing the primary colors.

Art Concept: Secondary Colors. Orange, purple, and green are made by mixing equal amounts of the primary colors, red, blue, and yellow

Materials.   Pencils
            Red, yellow, and blue
                paint
            Paper
            Brushes
            Paint dishes

Instructions.

1. Direct students to draw with pencil a house, and trees.

2. In a paint dish, begin mixing the primary colors in equal amounts to make the secondary colors.

3. Paint the picture using the secondary colors, but leave the areas white where the snow should be.

Tuesday
By David Wiesner
(New York: Clarion Books, 1991)
1992 Caldecott Award Winner

Frogs rise on their lily pads, float through the air, and explore
the nearby houses while the inhabitants sleep.

Night Scene

Notice the colors the artist used to convey to the viewer that the action occurs at night. Working with the colors black, white, and blue, the students may make tints and shades of blue to create a night scene.

Art Concepts:

Tint. Color plus white

Shade. Color plus black

Materials. Drawing paper
Pencils
Black, white, and blue
paint
Paint dishes
Brushes

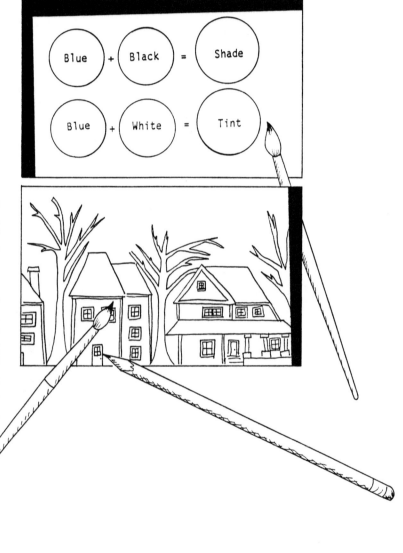

Instructions.

1. Demonstrate mixing colors for the class. Begin with a pure color and gradually add small amounts of black or white to show the color variations.

2. Instruct students to draw with pencil the skyline of a town. When students have completed their drawing, they should begin to paint using tints and shades of blue. If desired, frogs may be added to the painting by following the step-by-step instructions in the Pencil chapter on page 15.

White Snow, Bright Snow
Illustrated by Roger Duvoisin
Written by Alvin Tresselt
(New York: Lothrop, Lee & Shepard, 1947)
1948 Caldecott Award Winner

A snowfall shows the difference in reactions between children and adults.

Houses in the Snow
To give the houses form, the artist painted the sides darker, which gives the appearance of a shaded area. Students may do this by mixing black into the pure color.

Art Concept: Shade. A color mixed with black

Materials. White paper
Paint
Pencils
Brushes
Paint dishes

Instructions.
1. Direct students to draw a variety of houses on white paper using pencil. First paint the fronts of the houses with the pure colors.

2. In a paint dish, mix black into the pure color and paint the sides of the houses and details such as windows and doors. Keep areas of the paper white to show snow.

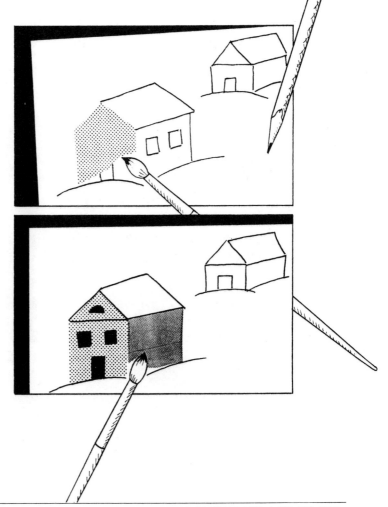

Chapter
11

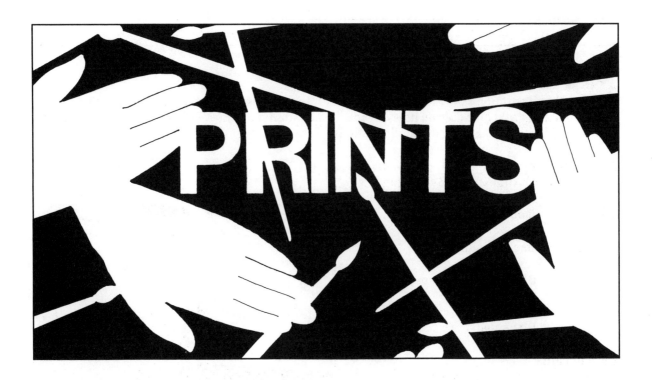

This chapter provides a variety of lessons that explore print-making. Printmaking is the process of transferring paint or ink from one surface to another surface such as paper. Two main printing techniques are used: raised surface printing and mono-prints. Raised surface printing uses materials such as thick paper, Styrofoam, cardboard, oak tag, and glue to provide an area that is slightly higher than the background. Paint applied to the raised surface may be transferred to another surface to make multiple images. Monoprints are made by applying paint to a nonporous surface and pressing a sheet of paper into the design to transfer the image.

Baboushka and the Three Kings
Illustrated by Nicolas Sidjakov
Written by Ruth Robbins
(Berkeley, Calif.: Parnassus, 1960)
1961 Caldecott Award Winner

A Russian legend about a woman and her search for the Christ child.

Trees in the Snow

Examine the illustration as the travelers disappear into the snow. Crayon rubbed over the surface of a paper that has dried glue dots on it has an appearance similar to snow. Using markers, students may draw trees similar to the trees in the illustrations.

Art Concept: Glue Print. A dried glue image can be transferred by rubbing crayon over the surface of a paper that has been placed on top of the glue image.

Materials. Background paper for glue
Blue construction paper
Glue
White crayons
Black markers

Instructions.
1. Ask students to place small dots of glue on the background paper. Open the glue bottles slightly so that only a small amount of glue flows out.

2. Once the glue has dried completely, place the blue construction paper over the dried glue. Using the side of a peeled white crayon, rub over the entire surface.

3. Draw the trees using black markers.

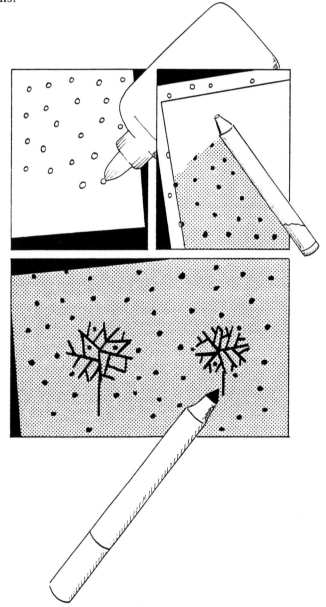

Finders Keepers
Illustrated by Nicolas [Nicolas Mordvinoff]
Written by Will [William Lipkind]
(New York: Harcourt, Brace, 1951)
1952 Caldecott Award Winner

Two dogs find a bone and learn a lesson about sharing.

Dog Prints

To achieve a bold image of a dog similar to the ones in the book, students may use a method of printmaking with cardboard.

Art Concept: Cardboard Print. A shape cut from cardboard and glued to a background is coated with paint, which is transferred to a piece of paper by placing the paper over the wet image. Many prints can be made by repainting the cardboard image.

Materials. Paper for printing
Pencils
Thin cardboard that cuts
easily with scissors
Scissors
Paint
Brushes
Scrap paper
Paint dishes

Instructions.

1. Ask students to draw the outline of a dog on cardboard. Keep the shapes simple. Cut the shape out and place it on a piece of scrap paper.

2. Using a brush, coat the surface of the cardboard with paint.

3. Lay a piece of paper over the painted image and rub the back of the paper. Carefully remove the paper and repeat by applying more paint to the cardboard image.

From *Art Through Children's Literature*. ©1994. Teacher Ideas Press, P.O. Box 6633, Englewood, CO 80155-6633, 1-800-237-6124.

The Funny Little Woman

Illustrated by Blair Lent
Retold by Arlene Mosel
(New York: Dutton, 1972)
1973 Caldecott Award Winner

A Japanese woman follows a rice dumpling into a hole in the ground
where she encounters a wicked Oni.

Line Prints

Different types of lines are used to describe objects in the pictures. Smooth lines are used for buildings and rocks, and wide ragged lines are used for roots. Dots are used to indicate soil and sand, and groups of curved lines are used for water. Students may draw a variety of lines into Styrofoam to make a print of the world of the Oni.

Art Concept: Lines. Different types of lines can be used to describe various objects

Materials. Pencils
Styrofoam from fruit or
    meat trays
Paint
Brushes
Paint dishes
Paper

Instructions.

1. Provide each student with a piece of Styrofoam. Using a pencil and pressing heavily the students should draw a picture of the world of the Oni. Point out to the class that they should use lines that suggest the object they are making, such as ragged lines for roots.

2. Have students coat the surface of the Styrofoam with paint. Lay a piece of paper on top of the paint and rub the back of the paper to transfer the image to the paper. Repeat the above steps to make additional pictures.

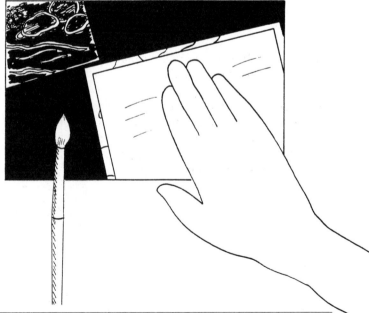

From *Art Through Children's Literature*. ©1994. Teacher Ideas Press, P.O. Box 6633, Englewood, CO 80155-6633, 1-800-237-6124.

Once a Mouse
Illustrated and retold by Marcia Brown
(New York: Scribner, 1961)
1962 Caldecott Award Winner

A fable from India about a mouse that is rescued by a hermit.

Animal Print
Students may make many images of one animal by rubbing crayon over a paper that is placed over a cut out animal shape.

Art Concept: Rubbing Method. Placing a piece of paper over a shape cut from heavy paper and rubbing with the side of a crayon to transfer the image

Materials: Scraps of heavy paper or
               oak tag
               Paper for making prints
               Scissors
               Pencils
               Crayons

Instructions.
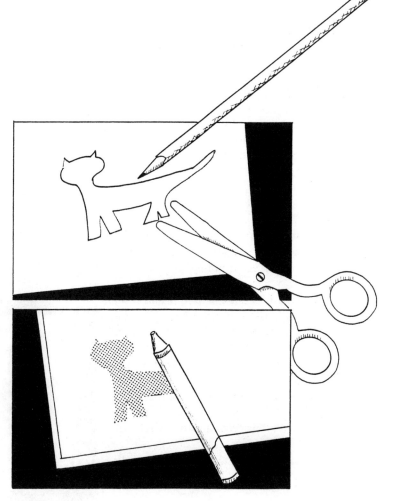

1. Ask students to select an animal from the story and draw it with pencil on the oak-tag paper or heavy paper. Keep the shape simple. Cut out the animal.

2. Lay a piece of paper over the animal shape and rub, pressing hard with the side of a peeled crayon. The shape can be moved around and rubbed several times on one sheet with different colors. Repeat the above steps with additional sheets of paper.

Once a Mouse
Illustrated and retold by Marcia Brown
(New York: Scribner, 1961)
1962 Caldecott Award Winner

A fable from India about a mouse that is rescued by a hermit.

Crayon Rubbings on a Raised-Glue Surface

The artist uses the technique of printmaking to produce the artwork. By using this method the artist can make many copies of one design. There are many types of printmaking methods, but the raised-glue method is a simple process.

Art Concept: Raised-Glue Printmaking. Rubbing crayon over a piece of paper that has been laid over a design made from glue

Materials. Heavy paper for gluing
Paper for making prints
White glue
Pencils
Crayons

Instructions.

1. Ask students to pick an animal from the story. With pencil on the heavy paper, draw the basic shape of the animal, but leave out the small details.

2. Trace over the pencil lines with a thin stream of glue, and let the glue dry for several hours.

3. Take a piece of the paper and lay it on top of the dried-glue design. Then with the side of a peeled crayon press hard and rub the crayon over the surface of the paper. The image of the animal should appear on the paper. Remove the paper and repeat the above steps with another sheet.

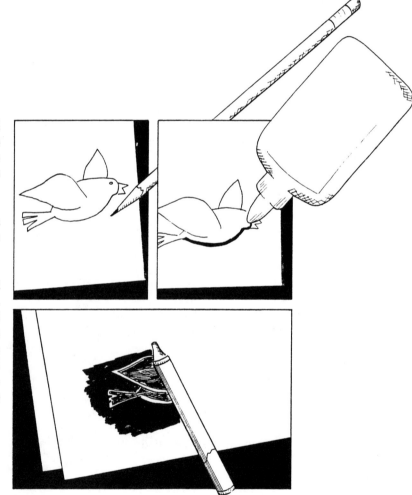

Sam, Bangs & Moonshine
Illustrated and written by Evaline Ness
(New York: Holt, Rinehart & Winston, 1966)
1967 Caldecott Award Winner

Sam, a fisherman's daughter, learns the difference between the truth and tall tales.

Cat in the Window

Using the technique of monoprints, students may make a picture of Bangs sitting in a window.

Art Concept: Monoprint. Technique for making one image. Printmaking with other techniques provide the artist with many prints of one image, but with monoprints the image is meant to be one of a kind.

Materials. Smooth, nonporous surface such as a desktop
Paper
Paint
Brushes
Sponges

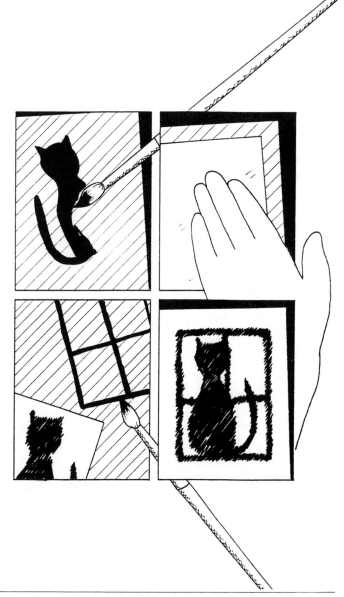

Instructions.

1. Using a paintbrush, have students paint the shape of a cat on the smooth surface, but instruct them to draw the cat in a size that is appropriate for the paper that will be used.

2. Place the paper on top of the wet cat image. Rub the back of the paper to transfer the image onto it.

3. Remove the paper, wipe the smooth surface clean, and paint the shape of a window using a different color.

4. Place the paper with the cat image on top of the wet window and rub the back of the paper. Remove the paper and let the images dry. Another picture can be made by repeating the process.

Sam, Bangs & Moonshine
Illustrated and written by Evaline Ness
(New York: Holt, Rinehart & Winston, 1966)
1967 Caldecott Award Winner

Sam, a fisherman's daughter, learns the difference between the truth and tall tales.

Lighthouse Print
Students may combine drawing and printmaking to create a picture similar to the illustration in the story of the lighthouse and the moon.

Art Concept: Monoprint and Drawing. The two techniques may be combined to make an image

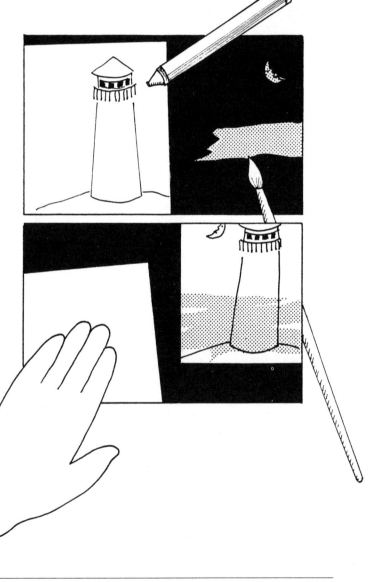

Materials.   Nonporous surface
Paper
Paint
Crayons
Brushes

Instructions.
1. Direct students to draw the shape of a lighthouse on several sheets of paper with crayon. Then paint a background and moon on the non-porous surface with a brush.

2. Place one of the drawings of the lighthouse on the wet paint and rub the back of the paper to transfer the image. Wipe the painted surface clean and repeat the above steps.

Sam, Bangs & Moonshine
Illustrated and written by Evaline Ness
(New York: Holt, Rinehart & Winston, 1966)
1967 Caldecott Award Winner

Sam, a fisherman's daughter, learns the difference between the truth and tall tales.

String Print

In the story, examine the illustration of Sam as she imagines the dragons and note how the background appears to have string shapes that add to the dreamlike quality of the illustration. Students may add string to their monoprint to make a picture from their imagination.

Art Concept: Monoprint with String. String may be added to the painted surface of a monoprint to block out areas of the image

Materials.   Nonporous surface
Paper
Paint
Brushes
Sponges
String
Crayons

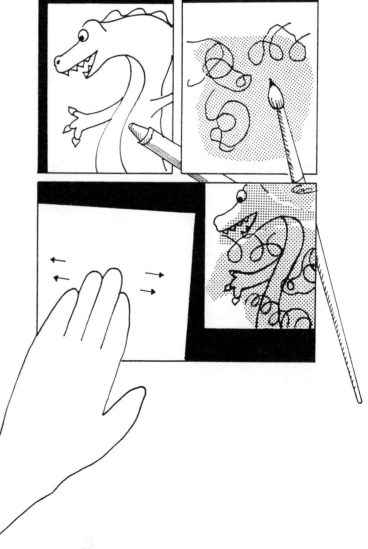

Instructions.

1. Ask students to begin by drawing an image from their imaginations on the paper with crayon.

2. Paint the nonporous surface, keeping the size smaller than the paper. Place pieces of string in the paint.

3. Then set the drawing facedown in the wet paint and rub the back of the paper to transfer the image onto it. Repeat the above steps to make additional prints.

From *Art Through Children's Literature*. ©1994. Teacher Ideas Press, P.O. Box 6633, Englewood, CO 80155-6633, 1-800-237-6124.

The Snowy Day
By Ezra Jack Keats
(New York: Viking, 1962)
1963 Caldecott Award Winner

The city where Peter lives is the setting for his day in the snow.

Snowflake Stamping

In the story Peter wakes up and finds that it is snowing. Notice the type of snowflakes the artist used in the illustration. Using hand-crafted stamps made from cardboard and paper, students may make a snowflake design.

Art Concept: Stamping. A printmaking technique

Materials. 2-x-2-inch corrugated
     cardboard
2-x-2-inch heavy paper
Scissors
Glue
Paint
Brushes
Paint dishes
Colored construction
     paper for printing
Masking tape
Paper towel

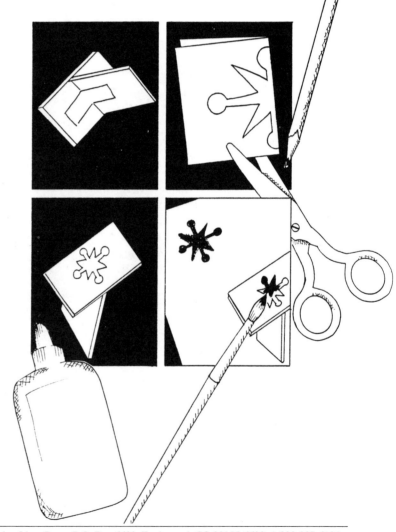

Instructions.

1. Provide each student with two pieces of cardboard. Instruct students to tape the pieces in the shape of a *T*.

2. Fold the 2-x-2-inch paper in half, and draw half of a simple snowflake. Cut the snowflake out.

3. Glue the snowflake to the cardboard.

4. Using a brush, paint the surface of the snowflake and stamp the image on the construction paper. Repeat by adding more paint to the snowflake. Use a paper towel to wipe excess paint off of the cardboard.

A Story A Story
Illustrated and retold by Gail E. Haley
(New York: Atheneum, 1970)
1971 Caldecott Award Winner

In order to receive a box of stories from the Sky God, Ananse must perform three tasks.

Hornet Print

Look at the illustration of the hornets as Ananse tricks them into flying into the gourd. The shape of the hornets is symmetrical. Using paper glued to a piece of cardboard, students may make prints of symmetrical hornets.

<u>**Art Concept: Symmetrical**</u>. The same on both sides of a central axis

<u>**Materials**</u>. Heavy drawing paper
Scissors
Glue
Paint
Brushes
Construction paper for
    printing
Cardboard for
    background
Pencils

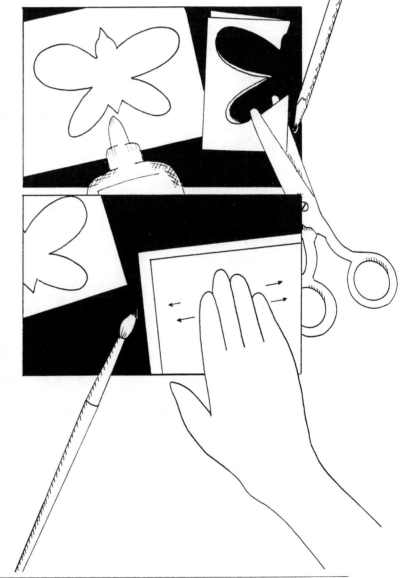

<u>Instructions</u>.

1. Fold the drawing paper in half and draw half of a hornet on the paper along the fold. Cut the hornet shape out and glue it onto heavy paper or cardboard.

2. Paint the surface of the hornet, then place the construction paper on top of the painted image and rub the back of the paper. Let the wet image dry before additional prints are made on the same paper. Another piece of paper may be used so that students may continue working while the paint on the first picture is drying.

A Story A Story
Illustrated and retold by Gail E. Haley
(New York: Atheneum, 1970)
1971 Caldecott Award Winner

In order to receive a box of stories from the Sky God, Ananse must perform three tasks.

Two-Color Figure Print

Look at the illustrations of the noblemen and villagers throughout the book. Using a simplified cardboard shape and two colors of paint, students may make a similar image.

Art Concept: Two-Color Print. Two colors are painted onto the printing surface to make an image

Materials. Scissors
Cardboard
Paper
Paint
Glue
Brushes
Paint dishes

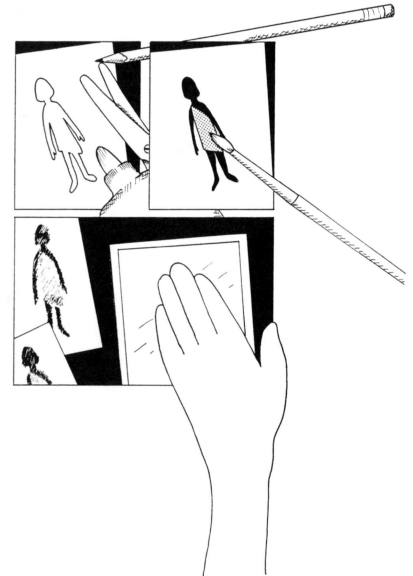

Instructions.
1. Have students draw and cut out a figure from a thin piece of cardboard. Glue the shape onto a background paper.

2. Apply two colors of paint to the figure.

3. Place a sheet of paper on top of the painted surface and rub the back of the paper to transfer the image. Repeat the above steps to make additional prints.

A Story A Story
Illustrated and retold by Gail E. Haley
(New York: Atheneum, 1970)
1971 Caldecott Award Winner

In order to receive a box of stories from the Sky God, Ananse must perform three tasks.

Web Print
Examine the illustration of the web that Ananse spun around Osebo. By using a Styrofoam print, students may make an image of a web.

Art Concept: Printmaking on Styrofoam. The surface of a piece of Styrofoam from a meat or fruit tray may be used as a surface for making a number of prints from one image. An image is pressed into the surface with a pencil. The surface is coated with paint, and when a sheet of paper is placed over the paint, the paint transfers to the paper except in the areas that have been drawn.

<u>Materials</u>. Styrofoam trays for meat
        or fruit
Pencils
White paper cut to the
        size of the tray
Paint
Brushes
Paint dishes

<u>Instructions</u>.
1. Provide each student with a pencil and a Styrofoam tray. Ask students to draw a web on the Styrofoam, but instruct them to press hard to make a deep impression. Paint the surface of the Styrofoam.

2. Place a piece of paper on top of the painted tray and rub the back of the paper to transfer the image. Additional prints may be made by repeating the painting and rubbing process.

Sylvester and the Magic Pebble
By William Steig
(New York: Simon & Schuster, 1969)
1970 Caldecott Award Winner

In a moment of fright, Sylvester the donkey asks his magic pebble to turn him into a rock, but then cannot hold the pebble to wish himself back to normal again.

Changing Seasons

Notice the illustrations in the story that show the changing seasons. Color is used to show these changes. Students may use a Styrofoam print to make illustrations of Sylvester as a rock.

Art Concept: Color Scheme. Dominant colors used in a picture

<u>Materials</u>. Styrofoam trays for meat
or fruit
Pencils
Sheets of construction
paper cut to the
size of the tray
Paint
Brushes
Paint dishes

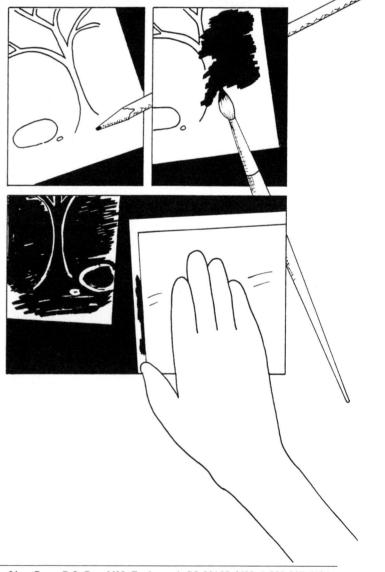

Instructions.
1. Discuss with students the colors that describe different seasons. Provide each student with a Styrofoam tray and a pencil, and begin by drawing Sylvester and the pebble on the Styrofoam. The students should be instructed to press hard as they draw to make a deep impression. Next add trees to the picture.

2. Paint the Styrofoam surface with the color paint that describes a season.

3. Then place a piece of construction paper on the painted surface and rub the back of the paper to transfer the image onto the paper. Have students make additional prints with colors that show the various seasons.

White Snow, Bright Snow
Illustrated by Roger Duvoisin
Written by Alvin Tresselt
(New York: Lothrop, Lee & Shepard, 1947)
1948 Caldecott Award Winner

A snowfall shows the difference in reactions between children and adults.

Monoprint Snow Painting

Using the monoprint technique, students may make a picture of a snow scene.

Art Concept: Monoprint. Paint is applied to a smooth, nonporous surface and transferred to a piece of paper while wet to make a single, one-of-a-kind print

<u>Materials</u>. Smooth, nonporous
surface
White and red paint
Black construction paper
Brushes
Paint dishes
Sponges

<u>Instructions</u>.

1. A smooth, nonporous surface is needed for this project. A sheet of acetate or a smooth desktop will work. Using a brush, have students paint a house and trees in the snow with red and white paint.

2. While the paint is still wet, place a sheet of black paper over the image and rub the back of the paper to transfer the image. Remove the paper carefully. Additional prints may be made by wiping the smooth surface clean and repeating the process.

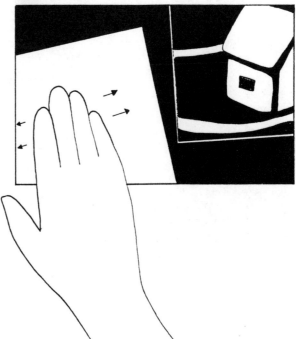

Appendix:
Caldecott Award Winners
1938-1994

1938 Award
Animals of the Bible, A Picture Book
Text selected by Helen Dean Fish
Illustrated by Dorothy P. Lathrop

1939 Award
Mei Li
Written and illustrated by Thomas Handforth

1940 Award
Abraham Lincoln
Written and illustrated by Ingri and Edgar Parin d'Aulaire

1941 Award
They Were Strong and Good
Written and illustrated by Robert Lawson

1942 Award
Make Way for Ducklings
Written and illustrated by Robert McCloskey

1943 Award
The Little House
Written and illustrated by Virginia Lee Burton

1944 Award
Many Moons
Written by James Thurber
Illustrated by Louis Slobodkin

1945 Award
Prayer for a Child
Written by Rachel Field
Illustrated by Elizabeth Orton Jones

1946 Award
The Rooster Crows
Written and illustrated by Maud and Miska Petersham

1947 Award

The Little Island
Written by Golden MacDonald, pseud. [Margaret Wise Brown]
Illustrated by Leonard Weisgard

1948 Award

White Snow, Bright Snow
Written by Alvin Tresselt
Illustrated by Roger Duvoisin

1949 Award

The Big Snow
Written and illustrated by Berta and Elmer Hader

1950 Award

Song of the Swallows
Written and illustrated by Leo Politi

1951 Award

The Egg Tree
Written and illustrated by Katherine Milhous

1952 Award

Finders Keepers
Written by Will [William Lipkind]
Illustrated by Nicholas [Nicolas Mordvinoff]

1953 Award

The Biggest Bear
Written and illustrated by Lynd Ward

1954 Award

Madeline's Rescue
Written and illustrated by Ludwig Bemelmans

1955 Award

Cinderella, or the Little Glass Slipper
Translated and illustrated by Marcia Brown
Written by Charles Perrault

1956 Award

Frog Went A-Courtin'
Retold by John Langstaff
Illustrated by Feodor Rojankovsky

1957 Award

A Tree Is Nice
Written by Janice Udry
Illustrated by Marc Simont

1958 Award
> *Time of Wonder*
> Written and illustrated by Robert McCloskey

1959 Award
> *Chanticleer and the Fox*
> Adapted and illustrated by Barbara Cooney

1960 Award
> *Nine Days to Christmas*
> Written by Marie Hall Ets and Aurora Labastida
> Illustrated by Marie Hall Ets

1961 Award
> *Baboushka and the Three Kings*
> Written by Ruth Robbins
> Illustrated by Nicholas Sidjakov

1962 Award
> *Once a Mouse*
> Retold and illustrated by Marcia Brown

1963 Award
> *The Snowy Day*
> Written and illustrated by Ezra Jack Keats

1964 Award
> *Where the Wild Things Are*
> Written and illustrated by Maurice Sendak

1965 Award
> *May I Bring a Friend?*
> Written by Beatrice Schenk de Regniers
> Illustrated by Beni Montresor

1966 Award
> *Always Room for One More*
> Written by Sorche Nic Leodhas, pseud. [Lechaire Alger]
> Illustrated by Nonny Hogrogian

1967 Award
> *Sam, Bangs & Moonshine*
> Written and illustrated by Evaline Ness

1968 Award
> *Drummer Hoff*
> Written by Barbara Emberley
> Illustrated by Ed Emberley

1969 Award

The Fool of the World and the Flying Ship
Retold by Arthur Ransome
Illustrated by Uri Shulevitz

1970 Award

Sylvester and the Magic Pebble
Written and illustrated by William Steig

1971 Award

A Story A Story
Retold and illustrated by Gail E. Haley

1972 Award

One Fine Day
Retold and illustrated by Nonny Hogrogian

1973 Award

The Funny Little Woman
Retold by Arlene Mosel
Illustrated by Blair Lent

1974 Award

Duffy and the Devil
Retold by Harve Zemach
Illustrated by Margot Zemach

1975 Award

Arrow to the Sun
Written and illustrated by Gerald McDermott

1976 Award

Why Mosquitoes Buzz in People's Ears
Retold by Verna Aardema
Illustrated by Leo and Diane Dillon

1977 Award

Ashanti to Zulu: African Traditions
Written by Margaret Musgrove
Illustrated by Leo and Diane Dillon

1978 Award

Noah's Ark
Written and illustrated by Peter Spier

1979 Award

The Girl Who Loved Wild Horses
Written and illustrated by Paul Goble

1980 Award
> *Ox-Cart Man*
> Written by Donald Hall
> Illustrated by Barbara Cooney

1981 Award
> *Fables*
> Written and illustrated by Arnold Lobel

1982 Award
> *Jumanji*
> Written and illustrated by Chris Van Allsburg

1983 Award
> *Shadow*
> Translated and illustrated by Marcia Brown
> Written by Blaise Cendrars

1984 Award
> *The Glorious Flight: Across the Channel with Louis Blériot*
> Written and illustrated by Alice and Martin Provensen

1985 Award
> *Saint George and the Dragon*
> Retold by Margaret Hodges
> Illustrated by Trina Schuart Hyman

1986 Award
> *The Polar Express*
> Written and illustrated by Chris Van Allsburg

1987 Award
> *Hey, Al*
> Written by Arthur Yorinks
> Illustrated by Richard Egielski

1988 Award
> *Owl Moon*
> Written by Jane Yolen
> Illustrated by John Schoenherr

1989 Award
> *Song and Dance Man*
> Written by Karen Ackerman
> Illustrated by Stephen Gammell

1990 Award
> *Lon Po Po: A Red-Riding Hood Story from China*
> Written and illustrated by Ed Young

1991 Award
 Black and White
 Written and illustrated by David Macaulay

1992 Award
 Tuesday
 Written and illustrated by David Wiesner

1993 Award
 Mirette on the High Wire
 Written and illustrated by Emily Arnold McCully

1994 Award
 Grandfather's Journey
 Written and illustrated by Allen Say

About the Author

Photo by Richard Lucas Photography.

Debi Englebaugh received her bachelor of fine arts degree in drawing from The Pennsylvania State University. She later received her art education certification and a master of arts in fibers from Edinboro University of Pennsylvania. She has ten years of teaching experience in art education in public and private schools at all grade levels. Debi is also a studio artist and currently works in a variety of areas that include bookbinding, drawing on handmade paper, weaving, and pottery. Debi lives in Mercer, Pennsylvania, with her husband, Robert, and two sons, Taylor and Morgan.